- Compliments

MW01104692

THE ORIGINAL-KING OF THE CAMPSITE

GINA L. BOLTON

authorHOUSE®

AuthorHouse™
1663 Liberty Drive, Suite 200
Bloomington, IN 47403
www.authorhouse.com
Phone: 1-800-839-8640

First published by AuthorHouse 4/14/2008

ISBN: 978-1-4343-2194-7 (e)
ISBN: 978-1-4343-2193-0 (sc)

Library of Congress Control Number: 2008901460

Printed in the United States of America
Bloomington, Indiana

This book is printed on acid-free paper.

"I travel not to go anywhere, but to go. I travel for travel's sake. The great affair is to move"   — Robert Louis Stevenson

"It is not the destination that is the reward. It is the journey" —
Lao Tzu

THIS BOOK IS A TRIBUTE TO MY FATHER ., THE ONE AND
ONLY ORIGINAL KING OF THE CAMPSITE.   1940-2007

I would like to say thank you to my mom, who told everyone in town her daughter was an author.

I would like to acknowledge my husband, Wade, and my sons ,Zack and Ryan. You gave me such wonderful memories to write about- thank you. I could never tell you enough how much I love you and thank you for never giving up on me. When everyone else doubted me, you kept believing. Thanks guys.

I would also like to acknowledge and thank my friends. Beth Farrer, Marilyn Petrie, and Merelin Angcaco. You are my big sisters, my heroines, my ego boosters, and my best friends. There will never be enough words to tell you how blessed I feel to have you all in my life. You rejoiced with me when I was happy, and you ceased my worries with tea and cheesecake. I also want to say a special thank you to Tina Hall. Without your belief in me, I wouldn't have written this book.

I also want to say thank you to my favorite cousin, Mervin Pasay When I was young you taught me be about the person I wanted to be, now that I am an adult I realize I am that person because of your support, your kindness and your courage. I thank the Good Lord everyday that he had the common sense to make us family. I consider myself blessed for just knowing you.

A special thank you to the talented, Janella Angcaco, for providing my photo for the back of the book and arranging the front cover of the book as well. I appreciate all the effort you made for me. I would also like to thank Dale Wanechko, for providing the technical support when I asked for help because although I am a good writer, I am lousy with computers.

I would like to also acknowledge Ron Bowles, Joseph Fatton , Teri Watkins, Ashley Eller, and Jeremiah Murphy with AuthorHouse Publishing. Thank you for being so supportive, and helpful and making the publishing process so very pleasant. My apologies to anyone I left out. I think you are all terrific.

I swear the events of this book are absolutely true. Well…Almost true. What can I say? I'm a great storyteller.

CONTENTS

CHAPTER ONE

FAMILY INTRODUCTIONS

When I was a kid the teacher in school used to pass out these blank pieces of paper and on the top written in black marker was the question, "What did you do over your summer vacation?" When you're a kid it's hard to tell in sufficient detail all the marvelous things that can happen to you over two months. I mean how do you describe the feeling of the night chill against your skin as you slip to the outhouse washroom? The wonder of seeing mountains for the first time? When I was a young adult, I would get the same piece of paper, but with a different question: "Why are vacations so important?" Truth of the matter is I didn't know why they were important. I didn't get any taller, or fall in love, or buy a house, or become a superstar. Nothing dramatic over the summer changed me. I was just happy to go on vacation; who cares if it was important or not? The question once asked of me in my youth has finally caught up with me today. Now with age, wisdom, and life experience under my belt, I finally have an answer for the blank piece of paper. Why are vacations so important? Vacations are important because the person you are every day is not the person you are on a vacation. Life becomes routine. You get up, you brush your teeth, you comb your hair, you get dressed and eat breakfast, then you get in your vehicle and you go to work. Well, when you vacation, your life is set apart from the ordinary routine. You are a completely different person.

I had the opportunity to know my parents, not just as mom and dad, but as thinking, feeling, expressive people who are capable of doing and saying anything. When your home is surrounded by debt, decisions, responsibility, car payments, and battles with the schoolteacher, a vacation gives you a break from all that. I saw my parents laugh, play, relax, and be the people they really are.

1

Now stories cannot be told about one's family unless one introduces one's family. Luckily, I have one. My father, Gene (a former teacher), is a beef and grain farmer in a small town in Alberta, Canada. Dad loved his hometown. He was born here. "Life is good here. Why would you want to leave?" he always told me. My dad also loves intellect. It was a plain and simple fact. My father's parents valued education and stressed it on their children. This serious love of education made life pretty difficult for us kids who just wanted to goof around and be kids. "Stupid kids," Dad often referred to us. In fact, I thought my name was Stupid Kid because it was used so often.

"Stupid kid. Hold that tire higher," Dad would growl at me.

"I am, Dad! I'm holding it as high as I can!" I would answer, as the muscles in my arms started to burn. I often imagined that one day my arm muscles would pop right through my shirt and fall out on the floor. Lifeless and bloody. Then I'd point to my poor twisted muscles just lying there in desperate need of love and understanding and Dad would feel so sorry for me. My face would be streaked with tears, and utter pain. Yeah, that would teach him.

"Come on, stupid kid. I said lift it higher," he'd bark at me again.

"I told you I can't lift it any higher than this."

"Ahh, give it to me," Dad would fume and grab the tire away from me.

"Can I go?" I give him my pouty look and my saddest eyes.

"Go," Dad would grumble. I would think my chores for lifting tires that are three sizes larger than me would be behind me and now I have a day of adventure ahead. I would just leave the garage when I heard my name called again under Dad's breath: "Stupid kid."

Besides my father's love of education, he also loved farming. My dad once told me, "True beauty is in a golden wheat field. A pasture full of quality cow stock, and a blue sky on a sunny day." I never thought so. I didn't know where beauty existed but I was pretty sure it wasn't with a herd of stinky cows. Cows lack a sense of humor and cannot be trained to dance like a horse. I know. I tried.

What was my discontent was my father's joy. He loved farming and dedicated all his time to this single career. "Too much time," mother would add. I remember my earliest days of childhood and how frightened I was of my father. He was a gentle giant, with brown hair, six feet in height, with soft brown eyes. He terrified me. You see, my dad would be already working in the field before any of us even crawled out of bed. While we were sleeping my dad would then return home with the dark and the shadows. We didn't know him. Once in a while we would encounter this strange man coming out of the bathroom in his underwear, and us kids would run screaming to our mother. It was at Mother's insistence that Dad spend more time with us kids, so we would know who he was or at the very least stop us kids from screaming whenever we saw him in the house.

My mother, Jane (former telephone operator, bus driver, housewife), was the yin to dad's yang. She completed him. When Dad didn't laugh, she made him laugh. When Dad didn't smile, she made him smile. When Dad didn't have time, she made him find the time.

Mom is Dad's opposite. Where Dad was tall, Mom was short. (She barely reaches five feet tall.) Dad had brown eyes, Mom's would flash a sparkle of green. Dad would smile, but Mom would laugh. It took me a few years to understand that Dad needed Mom not just to enjoy life, but to live.

Now the word "Family" would not exist without the word "children." Patty is the first to get Mom and Dad's attention by being born two years before me. Patty is like Dad. She's a hard worker, serious, and always seems too busy. Jamie is the youngest and the only boy. In fact, I thought Jamie's name was "The Boy," for that is how he was most often referred to. "Give the boy money for a ski trip," "Give the boy your pancake, he's hungry," "Give the boy the keys to the car, he wants to go out." It's a wonder Jamie didn't need therapy when his real name was used. Jamie is part Mom with a marvelous sense of humor, and part Dad with ambition to work hard.

Then there is me. I used to think I was adopted. I believed Cary Grant was my father and Doris Day was my mother. I had to be! I look nothing like these people. My sister and brother are tall, thin, and blond with green eyes. I am short, chubby, with brown hair, and the only family member with blue eyes. My sister used to tell everyone in school I was the milkman's daughter. In the school hallways I would hear the whispers about me and my real identity. I knew it! This explains so much. Why I look nothing like any of them and my intense love for white and chocolate milk.

"You are not," mother would tell me. "I'll talk to your sister"

"It's ok," I replied. "I don't mind. Maybe he's richer."

It was a shock when I looked at my birth certificate and realized I was the middle daughter of this family, like it or not.

Patty and Jamie are Dad's favorite children. They grew up to be the people he wanted them to be. They are smart, successful, and in the careers that he approved of. I was the disappointment of the family. I was not a Nobel Peace Prize winner, or a teacher, doctor, lawyer, or politician. I am an artist and writer. A hopelessly lost romantic and dreamer. I painted the world around me to express my sheer love for it and I wrote volumes of words to tell everyone what was in my heart. In short I was killing my father! He had such hopes for me. Even now when I look at his picture, I hear him screaming at me, "You're killing me! Stupid kid."

My family was a busy family. Farming took priority over all things. Farming was life. Education and school took priority over us children. Escaping school was our life. Mom made sure we all had priorities. This was her life. It seemed the only time we came together as a family was on holidays and church (which was every Sunday).

Every holiday started out the same way every year. Mom and Dad would plan a destination and a time limit. There was always a time limit. My father co-farmed with his little brother and all holiday schedules had to be equal. If we had four days off, they had four days off and vice versa. Every year there was a problem in the amount of days we had off.

"I just can't take all those days off," Dad would explain to Mom. "I have to help seed the field."

"I thought that you were finished with that," Mom would reply.

"I have about eighty acres left to seed," said Dad.

"Can't your brother do it?" Mom would question.

Dad would just stand there, chewing his bottom lip, and giving Mom this hopeless child look. He was in a corner. She had him. He had no excuse. The problem was never in the days we took off, it was that Dad couldn't leave the farm. It was like he was chained to it, and it would dissolve into dust without him.

"Fine, we'll go for seven days," Dad would grumble.

Seven days was the maximum time Dad would allow for any holidays. We all accepted Father's schedule proposal. It was a bonded verbal contract that he could not refute in any court.

With the excitement of a trip in the horizon, we began the planning.

Mom was the planner (I hate to tell you this, guys, but women usually are). Blankets for five people, pillows for five, enough food and water for seven days, jugs, milk, pot and pans, utensils, suitcases of clothes, jackets, shoes, tent, and tarp all packed into the trunk of our brown 1973 Dodge Polaris. I like to fondly refer to it as "the boat." Oh yes, the boat. Those tan and gold threaded seats are permanently imprinted in my memory with ABCs and all the words to "I'm a little teapot." I doubt if I'll ever forget them.

Now if it was understood that Mom was the planner, then Dad was the packer. In fact it was because of summer holidays that I found out that my dad was in possession of an extraordinary talent, for my dad (the man who didn't know who Siegfried and Roy are) is a marvelous packer. Despite the odds, my dad could pack half the contents of our home in the trunk of our car. (This is a skill that came in handy when us kids moved out.) Every milk carton, pop bottle, and pillow had a specific place in that trunk. I am still in awe of his skill today.

Besides the planner, Mom was also the checklist girl. Lights off? Check! Stove turned off? Check! Doors locked? Check! Was Jamie in the car? Check! Now you may think it absurd that a child has his own checklist, but accidentally it happened once that Jamie was left behind at a gas station (it was only a few minutes). No one saw Jamie get out of the vehicle and follow Dad into the gas station. We had just pulled out of the driveway when we realized that we were a family member short. When we turned around to go back, we found Jamie still shopping in the store. He didn't even know we had left. Thank God there was no permanent damage on his psyche. After this incident, Jamie got his own checklist. With the house locked down (not even Santa could get in), we would make our first stop on our holidays. Five miles down the road to see Grandma. FIVE MILES DOWN THE ROAD! We didn't even pass the train tracks in the middle of town! It was agony to us kids! I mean we saw Grandma all the time! Every Sunday for church, every time she wanted her pills refilled; I mean, who were we kidding here?

"No, Dad!" we would whine from the back seat.

"It's rude to pass and not say goodbye," Dad would frown at us from the front seat.

With ants in our pants (not literally) we would yell a quick "Bye!" from the back seat and roll up the windows. All that was on our minds was the open road and adventure. Of course, Grandma would ruin all our plans by inviting us all inside the house for lunch and Dad would always accept.

"She went through so much trouble," Dad would explain to us kids. With sour expressions on our faces we would follow Dad up the sidewalk and into the small brick and stucco house.

My parents were killing us! Dial 911! Someone help! I heard of Chinese water torture, where drops of water repeatedly fell on your head until you were driven mad. Well, this was Grandma lunch torture. A little Polish grandma feeds you homemade head cheese and perogies until you burst. We ate without tasting the food, we gulped it down, we gorged ourselves on the jellied meat and steamed dumplings. Whatever it took, whatever the mission, we were willing to sacrifice and risk all we had and more if it meant that we could start our holidays or at the very least leave town before the sun set.

By the time we finished eating and hugging Grandma goodbye it felt like half the day was gone. What elation there was when we finally crossed over the train tracks and saw the "Welcome to Redwater" sign backwards in our rearview mirror. We were now a family on the open road, looking for adventure, whatever came our way. BORN TO BE WILD! Yeah, we could afford to be a little bit crazy, we were on holiday.

Somewhere outside of Edmonton Dad would stop for gas and

ice cream. This would become the routine of every holiday we would ever have. In addition to being a work-a-holic my father was also a candy-a-holic. Every Christmas we would go shopping in the city and buy those treasured gifts for our loved ones. Every year the question of, "Who wants to go with Mom? Who wants to go with Dad?" would inevitably pop up. Us kids always picked Dad. We knew Dad would hit every hot dog, ice cream, fudge, chocolate, candy cane, baked goods, and milkshake stand in the mall. If the mall had a grocery store Dad would load up in the bulk aisles with nuts, peppermint, toffee, chocolate, cookies, chips, and every other hard candy he would feast his greedy little eyes on. Who needed a turkey with stuffing? We had licorice! Who needed to peel potatoes? We had pecan butter toffee! By the time Mom caught up with us we were all so stoned on gumdrops and chocolate-covered raisins she couldn't do a thing with us. Maybe it was a blessing to Mom, though. She got to do her shopping in peace and quiet, and on the way home we would fall asleep from the crash of sugar.

So you see it was never a surprise when Dad would come out of the store holding two shopping bags loaded with goodies. It was expected. A 2L of vanilla ice cream, grape pop, chips, cheese spread crackers, peanuts, licorice, and peppermint candies carefully wedged between Mom and Dad in the front seat. An hour later we would pull over and enjoy a warm, creamy grape float. (I say warm and creamy, because ice cream never packs well in a cooler with no ice.) Us kids didn't care! We usually only had ice cream at Christmas. (I won't go over the whole mall story again.) So to get something cool and sweet on a hot summer's day was a welcome surprise to us all. The summer sun was relentless on ice cream and on fathers who were watching the ice cream melt.

"Hurry up! Eat it! I didn't pay good money for it to go to waste!" Dad would yell at us. My dad was born in 1940, the tail end of the Depression. Through the experiences of his parents, Dad was taught to waste nothing. He learnt it well. Really well.

"So the cheese has a little mold on it, just cut around that part! Eat the mold on the bread, it won't kill you. It's only penicillin! It'll cure any sickness you have before you get it," Dad would try to enlighten us kids.

"But we don't have any sickness," Jamie would reply and make a scrunched up face.

"See, it's working!" Dad would exclaim, and by way of demonstration he would then eat the bread, mold and all.

Like I said, nothing was wasted in my family and certainly not creamy ice cream floats. Mom would search the trunk for five plastic glasses and spoons. Us kids would then pack our glasses full of ice cream and add just a little grape pop to make it seem that we were eating a float and not just a glass of ice cream.

"Mmmmmm, this tastes good," was usually the sound my family made while enjoying the summer treat. Now one float is heavenly and makes you want to taste another one. Two floats were filling. Three ice creams floats didn't make you feel so good.

"Come on, you have to eat it all up!" Dad would again yell at us, as he filled us all with another glass of ice cream. The fourth ice cream made you feel lightheaded. The fifth float was really just too much, that one had you running for the bathroom.

Then with everyone bloated, burping, and holding their stomach, we finally made our way back onto the open highway. These ice cream float sessions always made me feel like I was five years old again and having lunch with my grandparents in a restaurant.

"What would you girls like to eat?" my grandma would ask me and my sister. This was a gold mine for my sister and myself as we sat down on the red leather seats of the hotel restaurant. My father was never a big seller on restaurant food. His version of eating out was buying a loaf of bread and a roll of garlic sausage with cheese and throwing it into the back seat.

"Knock yourself out," he would tell us, like we were a pack of wolves waiting to get fed our next meal by the zookeeper. Yet here we were, two little girls and their grandma sitting in a real restaurant.

"A hamburger, fries, and a milkshake," we would answer our grandma as politely as we could without seeming over anxious.

When the food arrived we gobbled down all the food on our plates. Every last bite. Then the waiter came and removed all traces of our heavenly meal.

"Girls," grandma announced, "I have to go to the bathroom.

Please stay here, ok? Your grandpa will along shortly. So just stay here, ok?"

Of course a minute went by and Grandpa sat down at the table.

"So are you girls hungry?" he asked us.

"Yes," Patty and I answered.

"What would you girls like?" Grandpa questioned.

"A hamburger, fries, and a milkshake," we replied in unison.

I know. I know. You're probably wondering where two little girls put all the food. The truth is, I don't know. I mean I was five years old, for goodness sake! I just learnt the difference between my fingers and my toes. It was good food, but were we ever sick.

The fun and excitement of planning a holiday, packing the car, eating at Grandma's, and ice cream floats at the road side turnout would the be start of every holiday we ever had. Even when things changed a little (like when Grandma passed away), the routine and its order never altered.

Vacations with my family were always an adventure, but more importantly it became memories. Memories I am so grateful to have.

CHAPTER TWO

1977: MAGNUM P.I. AND COLD PANCAKES

I'm never really sure if anyone remembers the first time they go camping. That is to say, I can barely remember it myself. My father, it turns out, is a nomad when he's on holidays, a crazy gypsy on the loose. It was as if he had been released from the farm and resolved to see the world in seven days.

Our first holiday was to take place in the Rocky Mountains of Alberta. We made our first planned stopover in Hinton, only twenty minutes from the gate of the national park. I remember the sun had just crested over the mammoth grey-and-blue mountains as a resolved stillness was in the air. I had entered a Garden of Eden. Jutting rocks sliced through the white clouds and sent it drifting like mist across the sky. Tall, dark green pine trees covered the valley below. I have always loved trees. I felt they could speak to me. In a gentle breeze the rustling leaves were like a conversation over a cup of coffee in a quaint little bistro café. In a mighty wind there seemed to be a thousand voices that shout at me and commanded my attention. Even with no wind, the trees still had volumes to say to me in their silence.

Here I was, a lone soul in a valley of green giants that towered over me a hundred feet tall, and blinded me with their simplicity and honesty. Looking through the car window I would spy a quiet blue river that would lead to a spectacular waterfall or a gentle brook that would become a massive emerald lake. One system leading to another, one continuous chain that never resolved. How perfect this place was. A new world had opened to me and I felt in awe of such inspiring beauty. I admit I cried. I always cry when at the feet of splendor.

I remember my journey started with the uncomfortable feeling of waking up in the tent. There are only two words that I can use to describe what my first overnight tent experience was like: "cold" and "crowded." That was it in a nutshell. There is not much room in a tent built for four but holding five people. I was the odd person out and slept the entire night with my face pressed against the tent wall. In the morning the dew had collected on the tent and with my face pressed against it, the water had saturated my face and part of my sleeping bag. Still, I was glad to be the person on the outside and not the smashed sardine stuck in the middle.

Dad was the first to wiggle his way out of the sleeping bag trap and ventured outside to build a fire. Mom was next, to start the breakfast.

I opened one eye. My god, it was still dark outside. I slept in longer on a school morning. Who the hell were these people that they get up so early in the morning? We are supposed to sleep in and wait for the valet to pull out our luggage. Didn't these people know how to camp? I slipped out of my cocoon as soon as I smelled the bacon, pancakes, and hot cocoa cooking. Patty and I shivered against the damp morning as we searched through our suitcases for our clothes. I pulled my shirt over my head and arched my back as the cold t-shirt slid over my chest. This was insane! All my clothes had froze! Still the smell of breakfast gave me cause to dress quickly and find my way to the pine picnic table outside. It is amazing how food cooked over a campfire can taste so wonderful. I mean, I ate this food all the time and it never tasted this good.

Patty and I gulped down the food and then helped Mom wash the dishes and pass them to Dad so he could pack them in his organized car trunk. When you live on a farm, it is expected that there will be work chores and that certain responsibilities would be yours. For example, my chore was the garden. While camping, my chore would be shared with Patty. We were responsible for rolling up the sleeping bags and tent so that Dad could pack them up. There were no negotiations. No terms of agreement. This was our assignment; there would be no substitutions or trades. Only there was a slight problem. Jamie was still sleeping in the tent and wouldn't get out.

"Come on! Come on!" Dad yelled and clapped his hands over Jamie's head. "Breakfast time, kid."

Despite his honest attempts, Jamie never stirred. Apparently when we were all assigned chores, Jamie picked his own duty, which was to always sleep in no matter where he was. It was a chore Jamie did remarkably well, even into his adolescence. Jamie was profound in his craft.

"Ok, kid, you're not being funny. Get up!" Dad shouted and pulled on the tent flap.

Like I said, Jamie was good at his chore and remained asleep.

"Jamie, your breakfast is getting cold," Mom called out. "You better get up and eat it!"

Perhaps Jamie didn't like food, because he remained unthreatened.

"Jamie, get up or we'll pack up the tent with you in it," Mom would switch to threats.

Jamie closed his eyes tighter and rolled over as a deliberate statement that he will not be forced out his bed.

"That's it. Take the tent down," Dad gave the order.

"But what about Jamie?" I asked. Not that I really minded too much because I thought the whole idea of Jamie being stuck in a tent and packed into the back of the trunk was pretty funny.

"He'll come running out," Mom told me.

Patty and I giggled to ourselves as we pulled out the pegs and removed the tent poles. The big blue tent with the red roof came crashing to the forest floor. I imagined Jamie would come screaming out of the tent any minute, but to everyone's surprise he just kept sleeping. Apparently Jamie had a hearing problem and thought nothing of the tent crashing around him. This is no surprise to me that Jamie could possibly be hearing disabled, as it seems to be a contagious condition that plagues my entire family especially when work was involved; we all seemed to go deaf. No one seems to hear commands like "Take out the garbage," "Clean up your room," or "Help me with these grocery bags."

My sister would probably the first to tell you that I suffered the most. When I was five years old I went with my father for a ride to check the cattle in his combine. It was springtime and the manure had unfroze and made a soupy, stinky swamp all over the farm. It was impossible to walk anywhere, as the manure was over three feet high in some places. My father kept telling me to move to the back of the combine cab and stop stepping over the hole in the floor. Well, I didn't listen (this is where I contacted the hearing disability). I was busy swinging my leg over the hole and hanging onto the railing in front of me. It was inevitable that my father stopped short and I fell through the hole and into the three feet of soupy mess. I was rescued by my dad who really didn't want to touch me. I was told I was covered with the poop. It was in my eyes, my ears, my nose, and yes even my mouth. I was also told that my dad wrapped me up in a rag and took me home to my mother who gave me a shower with the garden hose and had to burn my clothes.

This story about my inability to listen to instructions is a firm reminder to every kid out there to always listen to your parents. There is a reason that they know better than you.

Well, the hearing disorder now suddenly hit Jamie even as us girls started to roll up the edges of the tent. Dad had enough. First he shook Jamie and spouted a few angry words and then realized that all the effort he was putting into this was not going to change the situation, so he decided to roll with it instead. Carefully grabbing the edges of a blanket he scooped Jamie up and threw him into the back of the rear window ledge. This left us free to pack up the rest of the camp.

Walking over to the table, Dad picked up the cold pancakes that Jamie never ate and threw them onto Jamie's chest.

"To feed the zombie," Dad winked at me.

I couldn't believe it; did my dad just wink at me? The man who commanded silence whenever the cattle prices or the news was being aired. The man who always frowned and yelled at me. The man who never laughed at a good joke. Is this possibly the same man? Yes, it was true. My father winked at me. Not only that but he smiled too. It was a miracle that us kids would always talk about.

Although it was early in the morning and all the other campers in the park were still fast asleep in their tents we made our way onto the highway. My dad drove with a serious frown on his face as he leaned one elbow out the car window, with the heater turned on low so the radiator wouldn't boil over. My mother had her window rolled down as well, with her elbow resting slightly on the edge. Her other hand shaded her eyes from the brilliant sun that just started to warm the earth. Patty and I were busy in the back seat watching the marvelous scenery pass us by with tired, dried eyes that we had propped up with imaginary toothpicks. The whole time we travelled down the highway, Jamie remained asleep in his blanket rolled up like a hotdog in the rear car window ledge (obviously it was before seat belts were mandatory), the cold, uneaten pancakes still resting on his chest.

This was to become the norm for us.

After a few miles past the national park gate we stopped in Jasper. The small alpine city has changed very little over the years. The town seems almost Bavarian in its décor as a Swedish influence graces the many buildings. Yet, there is a modest amount of log shops and lodges that pop up all over the town, giving it a mountain appeal. We never explored the many shops and businesses in town; Dad would never allow it. He was not the type of person who collected t-shirts, banners, or souvenirs from everyplace we traveled. They were, to him, frivolous items that held no practical use. Now food, that was practical. "You can't eat a t-shirt!" Dad would tell us as we passed the gift store. After a few years I learnt to rebel against Dad's views and respond with, "Yeah, but you can't wear a loaf of bread."

"You better stay here," Dad ordered Mom and us kids. "I'll be back as fast as I can." It would seem the grocery store was the only store Dad would tour. I decided to make myself comfortable because if Dad found the candy and bulk aisles in the store, we could be here for quite a while.

It was then I heard people pass our car snickering and pointing. I frowned at the rude tourists. I didn't know what their problem was, but really. So what if we're farmers? So what if we seem a little different; that didn't give them the right to be rude and laugh at us. A few minutes later three more campers passed the car pointing and laughing. As they got in front of the car one man turned to his two friends and laughed, "Is that cold pancakes on his chest?"

"I think so," a lady replied, and the three tourists walked up to the front of the store laughing even harder and occasionally looking back at our car. It was then that I realized that Jamie had become as much of a tourist attraction as the park was itself, like an entertaining animal in a zoo. Dad was gone for roughly thirty minutes, and in that fragment of time streams of people passed our car pointing and laughing at Jamie, still fast asleep with the cold pancakes on his chest. I never laughed. I thought of Jamie like a caterpillar. Eventually he would break out of his cocoon and feed on the nourishment left by his loving parents, like a small inchworm that devoured the leaves on our trees back home.

As freezing as the mornings seemed to be, by the afternoon the sun was in full force and you were melting. After a few years Patty and I had it down to perfected science, a complex mastery of precision planning that we had refined to a simple task. It was easy! At night, we would tuck our day clothes into our sleeping bags so that when we woke up our clothes would be warm against the chilly morning. Next there was the order of the clothing that you put on. First there was the t-shirt, shorts, and socks you planned to wear that day. Over this we would put on our sweatshirts and pants, complemented with a warm coat. As the sun warmed up the day, we would simply peel the heavy layers off and place them in the trunk of the car. In the evening as the night chilled the air, we would put our warm coats back on with our nightgowns tucked inside the jacket. When we got dressed for bed, the nightgown was warm against our skin and made a barrier against the cold sleeping bag.

Not only did Patty and I invent the mountain clothing system but we also invented the blanket air conditioner. When Dad opened the window the cool air just seemed to blast you, but if you put a blanket over yourself the cool air seemed to circulate around, giving you a much more comfortable ride. Unfortunately Dad never understood this new system.

"Are you cold?" Dad would ask us kids as he peered into the rear seat through his rearview mirror.

"No, Dad!" we would answer back.

"Then why do you have a blanket over your head?" Dad interrogated us.

"Because, it's cooler!" I would yell at him, but before any of us could explain the new air condition system Dad would roll the windows up.

"Dad please, roll down the windows," I would beg.

"I thought you were too cold?" Dad replied

"No, we're hot!" Patty argued, getting more than annoyed with Dad's ignorance against our new blanket arrangement.

My father would then roll down the windows and allow the cool, sweet alpine air come again rushing through the windows. Us kids wasted no time and lifted the blanket over our heads and accepted the chilly sensation as it seemed to mop away the sweat that threatened to consume us.

"Are you getting cold again?" Dad would inquire from the front seat.

However, before we could answer, Dad would again roll up the windows. We traveled our entire vacation with Dad rolling the windows up, and then down, then up and down again. Miles and miles of gorgeous scenery passed us with the car windows constantly rolling up and down. Poor Dad, he never did understand the blanket air conditioner hypothesis.

We visited many places on our travels. One of them that I can recall was Pyramid Lake. At that time, there were only a few cabins and a canoe rental shack on the main beach. Today there are hotels and paved roads with landscaped yards, a very posh luxury resort. Pyramid Lake was adequately named after the peeks of three mountains that seem to guard the lake; they resemble the pyramids of Giza.

We walked around the lake for only a few minutes when Dad announced, "Let's rent a canoe!"

I was thrilled. I wasn't even the least bit daunted by the fact the canoe was a worn out old rowboat. It would be my first boat ride, and I could barely contain my excitement. This event, however, did not impress Mom. My mother is an incredible bread maker, is a superb driver, and always wears the sweetest smelling perfume; however, my mother does not know how to swim. So when Dad asked her to join him in a rickety rowboat, she seemed less than charmed by his generous invitation.

"I'll go with you," Jamie chimed in and climbed into the boat before Dad could offer the invitation to anyone else.

"Fine, I'll go with the boy," Dad responded.

I helped Dad push the boat off the shore and let them drift a few minutes until they got the oars in place in the rings located on the edge of the boat. Hovering against the shoreline, I watched my father and Jamie sail across the crystal blue water in an effortless glide. Minutes seemed to lapse into hours as Jamie and Dad finally made their way back to the group; by this time dark clouds threatened the skies and made the water too choppy to paddle in. My excitement had turned to my utter disappointment as Dad cancelled any further boat excursions.

"No worries," Dad patted my shoulder. "We'll just go fishing instead."

Somehow, that didn't enthuse me as much as the thought of being in a boat on open water. I didn't know it then, but the desire to be on open water would haunt me for the rest of my life.

I tried to keep a stiff upper lip. I even went fishing, but it wasn't the same. I was so close to doing the coolest thing ever, something to brag to the kids at school about. Instead I went fishing for ten minutes and caught nothing but weeds before the rain clouds opened up above us and had us running from the downpour.

Damp and in a depressed mood, we drove back into Jasper. I love Jasper. It is the only place I know where the people are as eclectic as the buildings. It is a common sight to see tourists with their rope-climbing gear hanging around their shoulders as they sip a cup of coffee at the outdoor café, Chinese tourists passing them taking a thousand photos as if they were celebrities coming down the red carpet in Hollywood, and native Canadians in ceremonial dress buying milk in a small convenience store. Every walk of life all gathered peacefully in one place. In a religious aspect, it is a true example of cultural differences that display peaceful uniformity. To an unlearned farming kid, it was terrifying, all these strange people so different from the farming community I grew up in.

Located in the center streets were six-foot wooden garbage bears. Painted in dark brown with cartoonlike faces, they hid a flap in the stomach that you pushed open with your hand and deposited your waste. Every few blocks the bears stood on their back legs smiling at you with a sign to remember not to litter. Jamie was enchanted with them and insisted Mom take a group photo of us kids climbing on one.

"Oh great," Patty grumbled and combed out her blonde hair with her fingers. "What are people going to think when they see this?"

It seemed to me that Patty was forever concerned with the opinions and impressions from other people. I never knocked her for it; it was how Patty was made. I love my family. I know there are times when they seem cruel, uncaring, and dysfunctional, but when you love someone you take the good and the bad. With me, personally, I couldn't be bothered what other people think of me. I know I'm a good person and a good daughter. What concerned me was why, in such a stimulating place, Dad and Mom were not at all upset their son was attracted to garbage cans.

"As long as you know the truth, it doesn't matter what other people say," my dad often told us.

Baring Dad's advice I grabbed Patty by the waist and Jamie by a foot and posed for my first photo with a wooden bear. In a world full of prejudices, fear, and injustice I stood straight and tall, and smiled for the camera.

It was late in the afternoon when we made camp outside of Sunwapta Falls, just thirty minutes south of Jasper. Patty and I pulled out the tent and sleeping bags and rolled them out for the evening. Dad set up the fire while Mom went hunting in the trunk of the car for food. With skill that only a practiced hunter could acquire after many formal years of intense training, she whipped out a can of Chef Boyardee spaghetti and meatballs and opened the can.

Never before had us kids ever tasted food in a can. Raised on a farm, we ate fresh vegetables, milk straight from the cow, farm fresh eggs, and beef that we butchered ourselves. A meal in a can was foreign and alien to us. We never tasted Chef Boyardee, canned fruit, or canned stew, but with our parents' gentle reassurance that we would like it we sat down at the picnic table and let Mom scoop the food onto our plates. It was strange to taste meat as soft as the noodles but we decided it was not too bad, and we ate every last bite.

Just in case us kids didn't like the planned canned meals with varieties such as "chicken in a can" (and we didn't), "premade macaroni," or "canned prunes" (another winner chosen by Dad), packages of frozen hamburger and wieners were taken frozen out of the fridge. Now park wardens frown on this, apparently it has something to do with wildlife predators and their attraction to fresh meat. My father was never concerned with bears, not even with the large paw prints that left permanent pressed scars on the garbage bins in the campsite. My father would defy any large cougar to his rights to roll out fresh hamburgers on the picnic table and fry them in the frying pan. Having read all the tourist brochures and seen the pictures of mangled cars left by bears who went after campers' meat supplies, I was always disturbed by the amount of fresh meat left on the table.

"Aren't you going to clean off the table, Dad?" I frowned. "Aren't you scared of bears?"

"Ah, let them lick it off if they have a problem," Dad would ignore me and continue to fry his well-deserved burger.

I almost burst into tears. Bears terrified me. I didn't mind them licking the table for a few meager fragments of fresh hamburger; it was the thought that they might slip into my tent and keep licking that bothered me.

One memory concerning bears made a horrible impression on me that I never forgot. It was on one of our many trips to the mountains and we had stopped at a day camp for lunch. Just as we finished eating and began the task of cleaning up, a small bear cub came out of the bushes beside us. My family backed up and made our way to the safety of our car, all the while keeping our eyes on the little bear.

A foolish camper next to us decided to take photos of the cub, which frightened the little fur baby back into the forest. Whining, the bear ran back to a clearing behind the bushes. The wife called after her husband to come back, to please come back, but he was so engrossed with the cub and getting the perfect shot.

"Come on, kids," my dad told us soberly, "let's make a mile."

We finished cleaning up and piled into the car. An hour later the news came on the radio that a man taking photos of a small cub (in the campsite we just left an hour go) was mauled to death by its bear mother. This impressed me that we must respect the wildlife around us, be cautious, be even fearful, and maintain a distance but admire the body its life processes. To this day I never forget the clothes those people wore, or the look on his wife's face, begging her husband to please come back.

After a few overnight stops the routine of setting up camp and taking down camp became remarkably easy. As a treat for our hard work we were allowed to select a pop from the trunk of the car in the happy pop tray. There were so many different kinds to try, like "cream soda," "root beer," "Coke," "grape," "orange," and "ginger ale." Of course there was also strange pop in the tray as well, "grapefruit," "cranberry," and "prune" (we saved that one for Dad). Oh, but I remember the first time we opened the trunk of the car and saw the twenty different varieties. A choir dressed in white, with white wings playing golden harps, sang "Amen." The white clouds parted as the golden sun shone streams of golden light all around us. A single pure white dove settled up my shoulders. It was a sign that God was pleased. It was then us kids decided to drink the strange pops first and save the more familiar favorites for last.

After the strange supper of mushy spaghetti and fried burgers, and a grapefruit pop, we began the task of cleaning up for the night. One of the other tasks we preformed in this nightly ritual was the search for the water pump jack to refresh our water jug and wash the dishes. I still remain firm in my opinion that mountain water is the best tasting water I have ever had in my life.

While these basic tasks were being performed Jamie occupied himself with feeding the squirrels with little bits of bread from the table.

"I'm going to name him Magnum P.I.," Jamie told me, a name which was from a detective TV show in Hawaii starring Tom Selleck.

"What are you going to name that one?" I pointed to another squirrel fast approaching the table for a crumb of bread.

"Magnum P.I., number two," Jamie smiled at me.

By the time we left to go home that summer, Jamie had said goodbye to the last squirrel he had seen (goodbye, Magnum P.I. number 237, wherever you are).

It is at this point that my memory gets a little fuzzy as to where we actually travelled. I do remember we toured the Columbian Ice Fields (Dad and Jamie had a snowball fight by the parking lot), we hiked to see waterfalls (many, many waterfalls), and lakes (many, many lakes). Before we knew it the six days were up and we had to make our way home. Jamie waved goodbye to the mountains, then the trees, and the rocks on the side of the road, and lastly every blade of grass.

"Don't worry kids, we'll be back next year," Mom reassured us.

I looked back at the mountains as they became a picture that filled in the back window. I was now a true daughter of Eve, an outcast to the Garden of Eden. I closed my eyes and tried not to cry as I imagined the soldier-like angels waving their flaming swords preventing us from returning. I felt a piercing stab in my chest. I had been pierced by beauty and told to come back next year. Next year! That was 360 days to this date! I wished with all my heart my father never took me here. I didn't care if I never saw the farm again, I wanted to stay forever in this forest garden.

Dad drove the car to our last campsite, Abraham Lake. It was the last night to pitch a tent, our last night to eat a canned supper, our last night to huddle together around a blazing fire. We decided to make the most of every moment. With still enough daylight left Dad decided to try another cast for that elusive fish. Jamie and I grabbed the tackle boxes and prattled after Dad along the shoreline and over a hill to a quiet little bay, just perfect for fishing.

We weren't there for more than a few minutes when we heard a splash and a woman scream, "Ohhhh, that's so cold!"

A few moments later we heard another splash and a man scream in rebelliousness against the frigidly cold lake.

This was too much for Jamie and myself as we scrambled over the hill to investigate the disturbance coming from our noisy new neighbors.

We climbed the small hill and looked down at the scene before us and gasped. We looked at each other with complete and utter shock. We have just witnessed a mother of a bombshell and decided to include Dad in the observation. Swiftly as if our feet belonged to the Road Runner in a Bugs Bunny cartoon we raced down the hill to our father who was fishing below.

"Dad, Dad!" we yelled. "There's something you really should see!"

"Not now kids." My dad cast out his line and began reeling it back. "I'm busy."

"But Dad, you really should see this," I pleaded with my father, pulling on his arm.

"I said not now!" Dad growled at us and cast out his line again.

"But Dad, there's this couple over there and…," said Jamie.

"Not now!" Dad interrupted us, his face becoming red as he grew angrier.

"Dad, I really think you should come and see this," I looked back in the direction of the couple and all the splashing.

"Please, Dad, please!" Jamie insisted, pulling on Dad's arm, causing him to drop the fishing rod.

"Ok, ok. I'll come look, then you kids leave me alone and go play, ok?" Dad replied.

Jamie and I agreed and led Dad to the top of the hill. Dad gasped at the scene of the couple swimming off the shoreline below us without a single stitch of clothing on.

"You kids go help me pack up my rod, ok?" Dad spoke softly and retreated down the hill as silently as a deer.

We walked back to camp as if wild wolves were licking at our heels. The whole way back, Jamie and I bugged Dad for information.

"Why were those people naked?" we asked.

"Go ask your mother," Dad replied.

"No, you tell us," I insisted.

"I said, go ask your mother," Dad grunted and walked a little faster.

Jamie and I never did get Mom or Dad to answer our questions. I thought maybe they were too embarrassed to talk about sex with us kids. No, maybe it was because they didn't know what sex was? Yep, that was it! My parents couldn't talk about sex, because they never had sex before. It made perfect sense! My parents went to church every Sunday! They were devout Catholics! They were far too innocent and decent to know about the immoralities of sex. I decided to let the issue go and determined to one day tell my parents about the birds and bees. This way, they didn't have to feel embarrassed about it anymore and would feel comfortable enough to talk about it freely and openly.

This was our first summer vacation. I witnessed the beauty of the sun rising over the mountains, the whisper of the trees as I sat in the shade, I almost got to ride in a canoe, I had no idea where I was but I did a lot of walking, and I saw naked people in a lake. Not bad for our first time off the farm. I could hardly wait for next summer.

CHAPTER THREE

1978: DON'T JUMP, DAD!

Another vacation to the mountains; having remembered them from last year I was more than happy to go. The Rocky Mountains of Alberta are spectacular with many waterfalls, lush green pine rain forest, and crystal blue lakes and rivers. This utopia built by God's own hands is a marvel to mankind and generates billions of dollars a year through tourism.

It is not uncommon to see several buses stopped at a local gift and gas store with beautiful people from Germany, Sweden, or Asia get off the bus and start taking thousands of photos. It always gave me a sense of pride to know that Alberta possessed such a place that foreign countries wanted to see. I felt like an ambassador as I would politely nod and help them find the washrooms.

Of course, tourism and the money it generates never had to go up against someone like my dad.

"Good afternoon, sir," said the lady in the park gate booth as she smiled down at us in our car. "Are you just passing through?"

"Nope," Dad would reply and open his wallet.

"How many days, sir?"

"Six," said Dad.

"That'll be twenty dollars," the park lady smiled and held out her hand.

Us kids knew when something was bothersome to Dad because he had a small twitch that affected his head and neck. This strange phenomenon seemed to mostly reoccur whenever money was spent. In medical circles I believe it's called "El Cheapo" syndrome. In fact I do believe the medical condition may have first started with my dad, who disliked anything that would require the use of paper currency.

So when the park fee was twenty dollars and Dad started the quick little head and neck jerk, we knew the fee was too much in Dad's opinion and we were soon to hear about it. That was also part of the medical phenomenon, lengthy lectures.

"Geez, that's expensive!" said Dad as we drove down the highway. "I just can't believe that!"

"Yes, dear," Mom would reply passively.

In my opinion my mom was a smart lady. She had years of experience handling Dad and his medical condition of El Cheapo syndrome. Mom knew that in order to diffuse the situation the best course of act was to remain supportive and yet noncommittal and never argue.

"I mean for twenty dollars, you'd think the campsites would be free."

"Yes, dear," answered Mom.

"I mean, twenty dollars?! That's bloody ridiculous!" Dad spouted. "What the hell does that money go for anyways?"

"Oh, I don't know, maybe it goes for roads," said Mom as she opened a map and started pointing out the places of interest. This obvious tactic of distracting your mate is a good course of action that I highly recommend in most marriages that are likely to be involved in this type of situation. However, this maneuver never does well with someone like my dad.

"Roads! Roads!" Dad's face would turn flush and he would start to sputter. "This place makes millions of dollars a year. If the money was going into roads, then why are there so many damn potholes?"

"I don't know, dear," said Mom as she tried to turn her back on Dad to look out the window.

This is the part that plagues most doctors and scientists. They understand the involuntary reaction of the head and neck spasm that occurs when opening a wallet, but they don't fully understand the lengthy lectures that follow.

Us kids knew that Mom had made two mistakes. One, she gave Dad a response to his question. When he asked, "Where does the money go?" Mom was silly enough to respond with "Roads." Bad choice of answers; she should had said "Schools" or "Charities" (Dad would not argue with that). Not roads. Anything but roads! I mean he was driving on a road and could visually see the condition it was in. Her second mistake was when Dad asked, "Why are there so many potholes?" she answered with, "I don't know." This response only left her open for Father to enlighten her with a speech full of substantial information that nobody cared about. It would start out with politicians and taxpayers' money, then to corrupt individuals who rob the unfortunate, then to the immoralities of mankind, then how farming is the way of the future, and lastly it would end with how Mom's answer of "Roads" could never fit the equation of the billions of dollars that was used through tourism.

Poor Dad. It was years later that I read a tourism sign that pointed out the various ways that your dollar was used by the government. There were new stores, new campsites, new bridges and pathways, new schools, new businesses, better housing, and new roads. In fact, millions of dollars are spent every year to improve the highways, improve potholes, and even create highway rest stops. Unfortunately when I read the sign my dad was nowhere to be seen and was likely to have forgotten his speech that he made years ago.

We drove past Pocahontas Park with all the cute little log cabins. Nestled in the pine trees at the base of a mountain it was charming in a pioneering sort of way, yet it felt like a little bit of Switzerland. I always wanted to stay there, but Dad's El Cheapo syndrome got in the way of any such plans.

Finally we made our destination. Maligne Lake Campground was on the outskirts of the beautiful Maligne Canyon. The canyon itself was a small opening of roughly ten feet; the canyon depth, however, was a hundred-foot drop into icy, fast water that pumped gallons of water per second. Many foolish people have tried to jump the small canyon only to fall into the icy water below and drown. Now there is a wire fence that allows you to see the beauty of the water below without the fear that someone will try to leap to the other side.

Like all campers we did the camper's circle (that means you drive around the campsite looking for a suitable place to set up the tent for the night). Once selected and approved by a democracy vote we would pull in the car and begin with opening the trunk.

"The campsite this year was ten dollars a night; last year it was seven," grumbled Dad.

"Well, everything costs money, Gene," said Mom.

"At this rate, I'm going to run out of money," Dad examined his now lighter wallet.

"Gene, will you please try to relax?" sighed Mom.

"I am relaxed!" Dad started to wave his hands in the air. "Don't I look relaxed to you?!"

"Well...," replied Jamie as he frowned at Dad. Patty and I shook our heads at Jamie giving him the cut-off sign. We knew from personal experience as the older siblings that you never interrupt Dad when he's in the "Don't I look relaxed?" statement.

"Look at me! Do I look tense to you?" Dad strolled up to Mom, pressing his nose only inches away from her own. The veins on his forehead seemed to pop out and were turning purple.

"No, Gene. Not you, dear," smiled Mom softly. I noticed that Mom had a gentleness about her that could quiet a lion. In her soft, affectionate, and motherly voice she could make you feel guilty, sad, and disappointed in your own self without really having to utter a single word. I figured out it was the softness of her voice. I learnt it myself when I became a mother (I find it useful when I want my way with something).

It was evening time, and the sun was just starting to hide behind the mountains when we set up the tent, brought out the sleeping bags, and searched the trunk for our favorite canned foods to eat for supper. Within an hour, supper was cooking on a blazing fire, as the scent of the pine trees filled our senses. Dad's rage of fury was all but forgotten now, as he sat in quiet contemplation admiring the scenery around him.

"Geez, it's beautiful here," Dad would sigh, breathing in the crisp mountain air deep into his lungs.

"Yes, it is," I replied.

I was born in 1967, the age of rebelliousness and wisdom. It was a time when people fought for their right to have a voice, to be heard, to stop the violence of Vietnam, and engage in peace. There were political outbreaks, painted rainbows, and Woodstock. It was an age of creativity of man versus its destruction. I missed the whole movement as my parents were just simple farmers, but the message of being a hippie and glorifying the earth and not its wealth of money was something that I grew up with and firmly believe in. It was why I became an artist. I wanted to remember the earth that I saw. I wanted to capture it and hold onto it, before someone came along and tore it down for wealth and greed. My creativity and my hippie-type lifestyle was not a view my parents understood. They saw being a hippie as someone who never cuts their hair, lives off the land, and has a name like "Rainbow Dawn" or "Sunshine Rays." They never did understand that being a hippie is not the name or a look, it is a political opinion to rally for peace, to oppose injustices. In the mountains, the giant spruce trees with the brown soft needles that carpeted the forest floor felt that peace. There were gentle, brightly colored wildflowers that would peek out from under a pile of leaves. I wanted to be a voice that was heard more than ever. I wanted everyone in the world to feel the peace that I was experiencing right now, as I stood beside my dad and gazed upon a breathtaking view.

Slowly the night settled around the campsite. The sounds of fire crackling, axes chopping wood, and voices softly talking became a traveler's lullaby.

I lay in bed, my eyes wide open staring at the tent roof. I couldn't sleep. I was starting to learn who I was, what made me the way I was. I was starting to understand that I was different from the rest of my family. It frightened me. They came to enjoy a change of scenery and play on a family vacation. I came to belong in the world and be a part of the world.

I rolled over and looked at my family as they lay in stillness sleeping. They were all so much like each other in their thoughts, ideas, opinions, and revelations. Why wasn't I like them?

Something happens to you when you're growing up and find yourself. You travel a road that only you can go on. You are alone in a quest of discovery. Sometimes we lose our way and can't find our way back. Sometimes the road goes straight back home. I lay awake for hours in the darkness as the wind rushed through the leaves, wondering if my road would lead off into the arms of people who loved me, or rejected me. Knowing that there were no answers for the questions I was asking, I rolled onto my back and fell asleep.

The sun was barely cresting over the mountains, and Dad was already up and ready to start his vacation.

Patty and I were fed, the car was repacked, and Jamie once again was stuffed into the rear car window as we made our way back onto the highway.

In a blur we passed Medicine Lake, Sirdar Mountain, Pyramid Mountain, and Jasper. At Marmot Mountain we made our first stop. Unless we stopped for the night, we would rummage around in the trunk for frozen wieners or canned stew and would assemble a fire in which to cook on. However, for lunch there was only a short stop and you were on the road again. In light of these occasion, a sandwich (usually roast beef, sliced at home before we left) and a pop (and some candy from Dad's bag stuffed in the front seat) was found to be a sufficient meal before we pressed on again.

This lunch was different from our normal stop, eat, and go again periods. This lunch Dad was admiring the view and spied a gondola lifting up over our heads to the top of Marmot Mountain.

"Hey, who wants to go to the top of a mountain?" Dad's eyes sparkled as he turned to face us.

"We do!" Patty and I yelled back in unison.

"Great!" said Dad. "Let's pack up and get going."

With supersonic speed us girls were repacked, organized and ready to ride to the top of a mountain. There was a moment of panic as Dad turned on the ignition, a fleeting momentary thought that Dad might change his mind. "No, he wouldn't do that, would he?" Jamie, Patty, and I would exchange looks with each other in the back seat. Our fears were resolved as we parked the car in the parking lot across from the ticket booth.

After the usual exchange of politeness the question of how much for five tickets would surface.

"That'll be twelve dollars, sir," the young girl in the booth smiled at us.

"Fine," said Dad. His neck and head jerked as he opened his wallet.

Our tickets now securely in our clutches, we walked towards a small crowd of people as they stood waiting for the lift to return to the platform.

"Geez, twelve dollars," Dad's neck and head would twitch again.

"Oh, Gene. Try to relax, will you? Come on, this will be fun," said Mom.

"I am relaxed," Dad grumbled to himself. "Do I look upset? No. I'm not tense," Dad grumbled some more as he stepped into the empty lift.

Slowly and gently the gondola lifted away from the platform of people and rose above the clearing below us. In the distance we could see a line of trees that marked the beginning of the forest below. Effortlessly we lifted above the treetops and looked through the windows at the ground.

"What is this thing used for?" asked Jamie, as he gazed through the windows.

"It carries the skiers to the top of the mountain in the wintertime," said Mom.

"See! See! It's the off-season and we still had to pay money to ride this thing! It should be free!" yelled Dad.

"Oh, Gene," said Mom softly. "Please try to enjoy yourself, honey. Look at the marvelous view."

Dad stopped, and smiling back at Mom with lover's eyes, he

knew she was right. Dad turned and looked out the window.

"Geez, I didn't think it was so high up here," Dad frowned.

This is where I discovered my dad was afraid of heights. Mom first discovered it when they were on their honeymoon. They went to Vancouver Island and flew in a small tour plane over Victoria. According to Mom, she had to literally hang onto Dad the entire plane ride because he threatened to jump out the door. Apparently, thirteen years later, Dad hasn't changed much in that area.

"It's ok, dear," Mom smiled and patted Dad on the shoulder.

"You know, I see a path down there. I'll just jump down and I'll walk up and meet you," said Dad, as he rattled the bars that closed the doors.

"No, Gene," answered Mom. "First of all, that's a road, not a path, and second of all, we are over a hundred feet in the air, you can't just jump down."

"No, I can see it! It's a path! It's a path!" Dad rattled the bars again pinning the doors shut.

Below our feet we saw a ranger's truck driving up Dad's so-called path. Mom was right. It was logging road used by forest rangers and probably by the ski patrol in the wintertime.

"Please, Dad. Don't jump!" begged Jamie, as he held onto Dad's shirttail.

"Look, it's no big deal," Dad tried to reason. "It's just your perception, an optical illusion. It looks like it's farther than it really is, and wider than it really is because you are looking at it from above and not at ground level."

Jamie, Patty, and I watched the ranger's truck pass the gondola and climb the mountain. We tried as children to never disrespect our parents and never give them cause to be disappointed in us. We tried to always obey the Ten Commandments and paid careful consideration to the commandment that stated, "Thy shall obey thy father and mother." It was a rule that us children believed and honored (unless we found that obeying my father would find him splattered like a pancake in front of the ranger's truck). No matter what my dad thought, us kids felt he would make a poor car hood ornament. A course of military action had to be planned.

"Kids, bar the doors," Mom ordered. Apparently Mom was way ahead of us.

"Oh, now you're being ridiculous," Dad scoffed at us.

Ridiculous or not, Patty and I stood barring one door. Mom and Jamie stood in front of another. We felt it better be safe than sorry. In this case, better to save a dad than lose a dad.

My father was not a poster for safety. It was more than possible to see Dad as the poster for what not to do regarding safety. Like the time Dad chained a wooden table to the bucket of the loader to change the light in the yard or the time he stepped on the gas with the bucket still lifted up and tore down the top of the Mayday tree. I always thought he would learn his lesson in safety after the grain auger caught his wedding ring and almost chewed up his hand like a sausage. No, my dad was an extremist. He defied the laws of protection and well-being. He flirted with disaster and danger.

In fact, if my dad was a character on "Lost in Space," with the robot and the Robinson family who can't find their way home, the robot would run out of batteries following my dad, yelling "Danger, father! Danger, father!" Or maybe it would just get pissed off and let him crawl on the roof of the barn that had just collapsed with old age.

No, you had to take Dad seriously when he wanted to jump a hundred feet down to a road that he felt sure was only a path.

At the top of the mountain, there was restaurant, a gift shop, walking paths, and a marmot.

A marmot is a woodland animal that resembles both a gopher and a groundhog. (A chubby, round-bodied animal with a bushy tail and large front teeth.) I had never seen a marmot before, so when the animal befriended my dad for peanuts that he had hidden in his pocket, I became very excited. The marmot backed up and let out a slow, drawn-out whistle as a warning for Dad to stay off his territory, but when Dad fished out a peanut the little marmot was only to happy to come a little closer for us all to inspect him.

Ten years later I saw a campaign to save the marmots in a local library. They face certain extinction as man puts up new housing and urbanizes their woodland forests. The numbers are dwindling and their survival is bleak. I felt it prophetically true that the marmot would probably cease to exist in forty to fifty years. Already biologists find it a race against time to breed them and increase their numbers, but what chance do they ever have of survival unless man changes his ways? It will always be the creationist versus the destroyers. In the end, the creationist always loses. You see, there is no profit made from the survival of a marmot.

I thought back to the mountaintop, with my dad feeding the marmot, listening and laughing as it whistled to my dad to feed him some more peanuts and growling at Dad and throwing the discarded shells when he ran out. There is no way of knowing when you are in a wonderful moment until it's past. I wonder even now about that marmot on the top of Marmot Mountain. Did he or she survive to produce a new generation for other people to feed peanuts to? Or did the marmots become a ghost like other animals that found the road to extinction? Only pictures in a book to tell us that they were once there.

With only a restaurant (that you can't make use of because you ate before you went up the mountain), a gift shop (that my father didn't believe in spending money in), and a walkway that only went a hundred yards further up the slope of the mountain, there was relatively very little for us to do. So thirty minutes later, we rode the gondola back down the mountain with everyone taking a post close to the doors so Dad couldn't jump out.

"Ah, you're all ridiculous," Dad grunted as the gondola safely opened on the platform base.

A new sightseeing destination was a lake. Was it Emerald Lake or Lake Louise? It's hard to tell when you're speeding by at ninety miles an hour. Later there was a hiking trail, somewhere, I'm not sure where.

"What's up here?" Jamie asked as we started up another hiking trail.

"A waterfall, or something," said Mom. It was the "or something"

I was afraid of. How crazy are we to follow our parents who don't even know where they are going?

On the trail we passed travelers with small bells on their shoes. As they passed us the tinkling sound echoed through the trees. Looking at the feet of the people as they passed us, an older woman stopped and explained to me it was a preventive measure to keep away bears. I looked down at my own feet and that of my family. We were all without bells.

"Don't worry," Dad smiled at me. Obviously he could see my concern on my face. "If we run into any bears, we'll just feed them Jamie."

Jamie looked up at me, with his eyes as wide as dinner plates.

"But Dad, but Dad…," Jamie stuttered.

"We will not," Mom answered. "If anyone gets eaten by a bear, we'll offer your father."

Just to make sure that Mom keeps her word on this, we made sure Dad walked ahead of us.

It was a short walk of only fifteen minutes, around the bend, up a hill, through some trees, and there it was! A spectacular waterfall spilling over the grey rocks that jutted out the cliff below. The roar of the water was almost ear shattering. It sent your heart racing and your senses reeling. Magnificent!

This is where it all turns bad for me. When I was a little girl, I suffered with painful and frequent bladder infections. On my visits with the doctor a urine sample was always called for. In order to get the urine sample my mother would turn on the taps in the bathroom, hoping the rushing water would inspire me to pee. It did. And so, apparently, do all waterfalls.

"I have to go pee," I whispered to my mom as I started scanning the tree line for an outdoor washroom.

"Just go pee in the bush," said Mom.

"What if someone sees me?" I replied as I crossed my legs.

"I'll keep an eye out," promised Mom.

I frowned and looked at the sparse tree line. I had faith in my mom. I knew she was trustworthy enough to keep a sharp look out for me. It was hikers and bears that I had no faith in. What if they came up the trail? They could probably see more scenery than they bargained for.

"No, I'll hold it," I jumped up and down. In the end modesty always prevails.

When we finally made our way back to the car, I ran to the nearest toilet. (Needless to say, it was a relief.)

My family has a long history of pee problems. My father (alias "the poodle") has marked trees, rocks, ditches, and outhouses across Alberta and BC. Even my little brother had his fair share of pee troubles.

"Dad, I have to go!" Jamie once whined in the back seat.

"Aw, kid. We just left the house, why didn't you go then?" grunted Dad.

"I didn't have to go then," Jamie explained. "I have to go now!"

"Well, I don't know what you're going to do, boy. I'm not stopping. I guess you'll just have to pee out the window."

Right around here, I become confused. Did Dad just give Jamie permission to pee out the car window? Or was he being sarcastic? No matter. Jamie took Dad at face value and rolled down the car window, opened his jeans, and peed out the window as we went speeding down the road.

My sister and I started screaming as the golden, yellow liquid streamed slowly across the windows.

"He's peeing!" I shouted as I pointed to my baby brother using the car window as a urinal.

Dad looked up in the rearview window. "Oh crap," was all he said before he rested his forehead in his left hand and leaned against the window.

In fact my parents never said another word about Jamie peeing out the window. I guess they figured, what's done is done. You can't take it back now. The event, however, must have made an impression on them, because after that no matter where we were, Dad ALWAYS stopped for us kids when we said, "We have to go!"

Over the next seven days we ate blueberries in the bushes (unaware that bears were on the other side), we saw more lakes and rivers. We hiked to witness some more lovely waterfalls and stopped at all the points of interest. We swam at Miette Hot Springs and Radium Hot Springs, toured Jasper and Banff's grocery stores, hiked some more trails, and then went home. Like a blink of an eye, we found the car pointed north and we whizzed past Calgary, Red Deer, and Edmonton. Holidays were over for another year. I ran to my bedroom and opened my calendar. I marked it with another 360 days until we go back.

CHAPTER FOUR

1981: ADOLESCENSE AND TENT TRAILERS

Over the next five years we would journey every summer to the mountains. We bought groceries in Jasper and Banff, we threw snowballs at the Columbian Ice Fields, and listened to the train whistles blowing all night long in Golden, BC. We enjoyed ourselves at the Accordion German festival in Kimberly, BC (well, except Jamie. He had bored buns.), as well as camping in Valemont, Kootney Park, Yoho National Park, Invermere, Canal Flats, Skookumchuck, Ta Ta Creek, and Cranbrook.

In fact we had been to the mountains so many times, not only did we know where all the toilets were, but we got bored. Very, very bored.

One summer in addition to our usual camping supplies the list would also carry 100 plastic toy soldiers (brought by Jamie) and books (brought by Patty and myself).

Jamie wouldn't even look at the mountains anymore. He had his fill of cliffs and peaks. No longer was he interested in goats, elk, deer, and birds. Instead he played happily on the car floor raging wars with his plastic army. Every time we stopped for the night, we lost a few good men. Whenever we stopped at a gas station or grocery store, a few more soldiers lost their way. By the time we got home that summer, the bucket of 100 men dwindled down to 50. Somewhere between Jasper and Banff plastic men were questioned, "Do you dare to be all that you can be?" They responded, "YES SIR!" and promptly got lost coming back from the outhouse.

My sister and I made our time fly by with books. Wonderful, glorious books, a portal of imagination and creativity. Patty and I lost ourselves in "The Bobbsey Twins," "Nancy Drew," "Minnow Vail,"

"Little Women," and "The Hardy Boys." I had to read the Hardy Boys because I was set to marry one of them. It was a toss-up between the pretty boy, Shaun Cassidy, or the good looks of Parker Stevenson. No matter; I wasn't fussy. However, the toss-up was over when Shaun Cassidy produced a record. Yep, the pretty boy could sing! I listened to "Da-do-run-run" over and over again. (I'll tell you now, my husband looks nothing like Shaun Cassidy and he can't sing, but I wouldn't trade him for any Hardy Boy. Ever!)

The scenery would roll by us as Patty and I would curl up in the back seat reading our books, lost in worlds of love or mystery.

I am reminded of an episode in a Walt Disney cartoon when Donald Duck drives his nephews out to the country and catches them reading comic books. Well, if life was a Walt Disney cartoon, then my dad was Donald Duck.

"What?!" Dad squawked at us girls. (Honest, he really did sound like Donald Duck.) "I drove 400 miles for you to see the mountains and you're both in the back of the car reading books?!"

"We're bored," I whined.

"Bored? Bored? How can you be bored? This is the mountains!" exclaimed Dad as he pointed to the snow-capped peaks.

"We've seen it all before," Patty yawned and turned a page.

"I don't care!" Dad growled and ripped the books out of our hands and threw them on the car floor. "I drove all this way for you to see the mountains and you will look at them!"

Patty and I knew if we were ever going to finish our books in peace we had better play Dad's game. We climbed out of the back seat and looked at the scenery. As soon as Dad was back on the highway and distracted with driving, Patty and I picked up our books to find out if Nancy Drew figured out the hidden message in the bottle, or if Minnow Vail was going to eat an ice cream float with her boyfriend.

Once in a while Dad would see us reading in the rearview mirror. He never uttered another word. There was a sadness in his eyes, as he sighed and looked straight ahead and kept driving. He knew it was time for a change.

In 1981 everything did change. Out went the old four-man tent with the old blue walls and sagging red roof, and instead there was a new vacation item. A tent trailer.

Patty was now sixteen, I was now fourteen, and Jamie was now ten years of age; we simply needed more space.

It was an exciting day when Dad searched through the bargain finder magazine and brought home a 1973 Coleman tent trailer. It was rather charming inside when it was all set up: mini stove, mini fridge, sleeps six, lots of storage, and covered with rust–and-brown checkered cloth.

"Finally!" I thought to myself. "No more rolling up a tent, no more setting up bed linen, no more packing up, because we had a tent trailer! Yeah!"

How wrong I was. In fact, if anything, the only convenience that the tent trailer offered was now we had more space in the car. The first holiday we had with the tent trailer, it left me with my mouth gaping open when I realized the amount of the work involved in setting one up. The trailer had to be first put on jacks, to maintain an even floor, or the door wouldn't fit. Next you had to roll up the roof with a crank, then pull the beds out and lock them into place. Once everything was secure, you had to pull the canvas covers (which made the walls) over the beds and zip them up. Finally the door was put in and snapped into place.

Frankly, I thought the tent was less hassle, but the tent trailer was cute with its rustic curtains and table with benches. When it was set up it could fool you into thinking it was a real trailer.

Now that the tent trailer replaced the tent, our new Plymouth Reliant replaced the old brown Dodge.

Everything, it seemed, was changing. Even us children were changing. Patty and I were no longer little girls, we were young women. As all young women do, we were in search of young boys.

Out went sensible hiking boots and in went hairbrushes, make-up, face cleaner, bell-bottom jeans, halter-tops, big hoop earrings, and hair dryers (just in case we hit a bathroom with electricity). For me, there was something special in my suitcase. It was canvas paper and my acrylic paints. Somewhere over time I had become a painter. Out went Dad's boring Ukrainian Polka music, and in went our music: Pat Benatar, Dr. Hook, Blue Oyster Cult, and my sister's favorites, anything by Aldo Nova, Trooper, Loverboy, and Ozzy Osbourne.

Problem was Dad sat behind the wheel and had control of the radio, and he definitely did not share our taste in music.

"Ah, ah, ah. What garbage," said Dad as he turned the car radio off.

"Dad!" us girls shouted. "Turn it back on!"

"But it's garbage," grunted Dad and he promptly turned the radio to the "Ukrainian Hour." Now that's music," Dad smiled and tapped his fingers on the dash.

"It sucks," Patty sulked. "I hate that ping pong music." (Little did Patty know that she would grow up, marry a Ukrainian farmer, have four beautiful children, and enter them all into ping pong dancing lessons.)

"Well, it's my car and my radio," Dad would reply.

"Ping pong, ping pong. I don't even know what they're saying," Patty whined. "I hate that music."

The funny thing is no one in the whole car understood a single word of the "Ukrainian Hour." My great-grandparents came from Poland. When they immigrated to Canada, the officials told them they had too many Polish, they were now Ukrainian. Ever since that mixed-up day, my family has long held this delusional belief they are a culture that we do not belong to. It's true that some of the family know a few words or sentences of Ukrainian but it was lost to the younger generation. I always thought it hilarious that my dad would listen for hours to the "Ukrainian Hour" and yet when I asked him what are they singing about he'd tell me, "I don't know." It's ok, though, I often had the same problem when I went to church.

"I'm going to listen to what I want on my radio, which is in my car, which is by my seat, because I'm driving," quoted Dad.

"Gene," said Mom gently, "it's their holiday too. Let them

listen to their music." This selfless act from Mom would end the cold war of who listened to what on the radio.

Dad would grumble a little and turn the radio back to our rock station. Poor Dad, he would grumble and snort in the front seat all the while giving control to his little girls so they would be happy. After about thirty minutes the pressure would be too much and he would turn it back to the "Ukrainian Hour."

"Dumb Ukrainians," Patty leaned back in her seat and sulked. She wore on her face an expression of contempt for the entire world.

Yes, things had changed for everyone. Patty saw herself as a woman of the world, truly independent, rejecting everyone around her. This hurt me. I idolized Patty, she was the only female my age I had to learn from. I couldn't understand why she didn't want me around anymore. Jamie couldn't care less about any dumb old girls, he brought an ice cream pail full of Hot Wheels toy cars. Dad even changed that year. After years of vacationing in the mountains, Dad decided to go on The Great Alberta Tour.

The plan was to go to Buffalo Jump in Drumheller, then to Calgary, and all the way up to Hinton, Peace River, Lesser Slave Lake, and home again in six days.

Yep, the gypsy was loose again.

To this day my memory is only a vague recollection of places I have been to and places I would love to see.

"I would love to see Saskatchewan someday," I once told my mother.

"Oh, but you were there," said Mom. "Don't you remember?"

"No, when was it?" I questioned.

"Was it 1977 or 1978? No matter. Don't you remember climbing up that hill?"

"Mom, I've climbed thousands of hills. You have to give me a little more than that," I said.

"Remember we ended up in the town of Many Berries and

your brother was upset because they had no berries to eat in Many Berries?" Mom laughed.

"Nope, doesn't ring a bell. I just don't remember that vacation, and I don't remember being in Saskatchewan," I admitted.

One thing I do remember about The Great Alberta Tour was Patty's zone book. Alberta was divided by these different zones and when you stopped in the zone indicated in the book you had to go to the information booth and get it stamped. Complete the book and you got a prize. We never completed the book, but it kept us all busy.

Gosh, but I was jealous of Patty. Not only did she get the cool book to get stamped but she got all the beauty too. Patty was tall, thin, and blonde, everything a boy looked for in a girl. I was exactly the opposite. I had gotten a little chubby; my hair was chestnut red, curly, and frizzed all over the place; and I had a round little face. My mother thought it charming to give me the nickname of "Gina Burning Bush with the moon pie face." All the kids at school called me ugly, even the teachers told me I was a homely looking child. Patty was all sleek and lovely with her tiny halter tops and her small shorts and I hid. I wore a huge hat, which covered my ugly hair, large sunglasses, which covered my face, and baggy clothes to cover my body. I hated myself.

I didn't look like anyone in my family, and I didn't act like any of them either.

"You're so different," Patty often told me over the years, and I was. I felt it.

The first night we rolled into Drumheller, we were told by the park keeper to not place our boots or bed liner outside on the ground overnight.

"To prevent rattlesnakes from climbing in your boots," she told us.

Jamie and I looked at each other with a horrified expression on our faces. What kind of place did our parents bring us to? Did they not research this place before they decided to take us here?

"Make sure you also keep your tent closed at all times and be sure to check your sleeping bags before you get in them," the park lady said as she wished us a good night and walked away.

"We have a tent trailer, so the snakes can't get in there, right, Dad?" asked Jamie.

"They can still climb into the tent trailer, it's not that big of a step," Patty interrupted.

"But we have a locked door, and walls so they can't get in. Right, Dad?" Jamie frowned as he followed my dad to the car.

"Snakes can climb trees. They rap themselves around the branches and they drop on the roof. Then they'll slither down and find a little hole in the side of the wall and crawl inside while you're sleeping," Patty laughed.

"That's enough, Patty. You're frightening your brother," Mom scolded. "Jamie, the snakes can't get you because they don't like the taste of little boys. They only eat mice and insects."

That night we set up the tent trailer. Jamie and I huddled together on our bunk. Despite the reassuring words that Mom offered us, there was always the ten percent possibility that Patty was telling the truth and snakes would come any minute through a small hole in the side of the walls and bite us as we slept. A person has to always think about that ten percent possibility.

Needless to say, it was a restless night.

In the morning we drove past Calgary, or maybe I should say we flew past Calgary. My dad was in a hurry to make it to Hinton before supper. We drove past Airdrie, Didsbury, and Olds. At Rocky Mountain House we stopped for a quick lunch.

"We could drive straight up the road here and go past Nord Egg and into the national park, through the mountains and in Hinton. It should take us about five hours of straight driving," said Mom as she pointed her finger along the roads on the map.

"Nah, we'll take this shortcut here," said Dad as he pointed to a grey line on the map.

"Gene, that's a logging road. You can't take that."

"It's a shortcut. Look, it will only take us three and a half hours if we turn off at Nord Egg," explained Dad.

Jamie and I looked at each other with fear in our eyes. Did our dad just say "shortcut"?

Our father had a problem with shortcuts. He kept thinking he knew where they were. The problem was, in a strange place, Dad didn't even know where he was half the time.

Once a few years ago we traveled to the lovely Bavarian town of Kimberly, BC. We had hit a German music festival and decided to stay awhile. After a few days we decided to pack up and move on.

"Gene, turn right when you reach the highway," Mom folded out the map.

"Nope. I know a shortcut," Dad said.

"How can you know a shortcut? You don't even know where you are," replied Mom. (See, I told you he didn't know where he was half the time.)

"I just do," Dad grumbled and turned the car left as he reached the highway.

Well, it was a twenty-minute drive up a long narrow service road that connected to a back gravel road, then a thirty-minute drive that connected to a pathway in a field that eventually placed us on hill overlooking the town on Kimberly below and absolutely nowhere near the highway. I remember that Mom gave Dad the "I told you so" look as she guided him back down to the highway again.

A time before that we were camping in Banff, just outside the Kootney National Park gates, when Dad decided to take a shortcut from a campsite. We ended up in a field with a log building and a pine fence around it. The house was abandoned with a wood floor and walls and there were no doors or windows. In the yard, there was tiny tepees all planted in a row with ribbons and beads on them. We got out and took a look around. On a small plaque on the wall, it said, "The Original Home of David Thompson, surveyor of the Rocky Mountains." The stories of David Thompson are legendary as a surveyor through the mountains for the CPR train in the 1800s. Here we were standing in the doorway of a legend. I don't know if I can describe the intense feelings I had right at that moment. This was not a museum display, this was his actual home. It was where he slept, and ate, and lived. I looked out the door and watched the mountains. David Thompson lived here and died here in the Rocky Mountains he came to love. He was a fortunate man. I walked out to the tiny tepees beside the cabin. I found a ribbon on the ground and placed it back on the tepee.

"What is this place?" I asked my mom.

"It's a native burial ground," explained Mom.

"Why do they have necklaces and ribbons all over them?"

"It is a gift to offer the dead," said Mom. "Now come back to the car. This place is sacred and we shouldn't be here."

It's true. We shouldn't have been there, but us kids all had to admit that of all the corny shortcuts that Dad took over the years, that one was the coolest. I looked back at the graveyard as we drove away. It was beautiful in a silent and peaceful way. Brightly colored ribbons floated in the wind like tiny butterflies to mark the place of a soul laid to rest.

Like I said, Dad had a problem with shortcuts.

"Gene, are you listening to me?" threatened Mom. "I said that road is a logging road. You can bottom out the car on a rough road like that."

"I will not," Dad spoke defiantly. "It's a perfectly good road, and since I'm driving that is the road we are going to take."

It was three and a half hours of the bumpiest road I've ever been on in my life. Dad remained true to his word as we settled into our campsite just before supper.

Hinton is a logging town with a paper mill in the river valley. The campsite we stayed at was on the back of the river surrounded by pine trees with a view of the mountains in the distance. After the tent trailer had been set up and everyone fed, we all slipped off to the walking trails to explore the area and walk off our supper. Everyone except me. I wandered out to the river, and finding a pretty view, I pulled out my paper, paints, and brushes. I had a little cup that I filled with river water and I began the pencil outline of the river and trees.

Painting has always been a fulfilling expression for me. I hold the brush in my hands and it becomes a part of my fingertips, like two puzzle pieces that, once joined, become a whole. I see the image that captures me, something that leave me breathless, then the signal from my brain goes to the fingertips as the brush glides over a white sheet. There have been times when the image haunts me, and I become obsessed with painting it. Only when that image has been created on my canvas, when my passion has been satisfied, can I be free of it and move on.

I dipped my brush into the dark green paint that would be the background for my forest, and then with my detail brush I added the small impressions that would be the foreground branches of the pine forest.

"If you add a dark highlight here and here, you'll get more depth in your forest," a male voice said behind me.

I looked up into the bluest eyes of the handsomest boy I had ever seen in my life. He was around seventeen, tall, slim in build, but had some muscles, with long slim legs. He wore a navy blue t-shirt and tan shorts. His hair was brown and feathered across his forehead. His face was maturing into a young man and he had a whisper of a moustache appearing under his nose. To me he looked like Parker Stevenson, the eldest of the Hardy Boys. I looked back to my painting and pulled my huge sunglasses back on the bridge of my nose.

"Mind if I sit and share your energy?" the boy spoke.

"All right," I answered shyly. I had no idea what he was talking about, but if he wanted to sit by me I didn't mind a bit.

"My name is Kevin," he smiled at me.

"I'm Gina," I said as I pulled my huge hat over my hair.

"So, what style do you paint?" asked Kevin as he pulled out his paper and brushes.

"I don't know," I said. It was true, I didn't know. I had no idea what art was, or what the art movement was all about. I only knew that when I had a brush in my hand I could paint.

"I'll tell you what. We'll just sit here and chat and paint and when we're done, I'll tell you what style you are, ok?" he smiled at me.

"Ok," I agreed.

It was the most amazing chat I ever had with a boy in my young life. Kevin and I painted in the evening sun, side by side; our hands held our brushes that danced across the paper. As we painted Kevin talked about artists I never heard of like Monet, Van Gogh, Michelangelo, Raphael, Rembrandt, and Picasso. Kevin recited poetry from Keats and Browning, even some of his own he made up. We talked about how art made us feel, the sights we've seen, the passion and heat we get from a well-executed picture. I felt intoxicated. I had never heard words like these before. I always felt alone in my world and here was a boy like me. It was like he could look right inside of me and understand me. I wanted to cry with joy, laugh out loud, and scream that I am reborn. I was no longer invisible. I was seen.

"I'll show you an easier way to make a background for your forest," Kevin offered as he dipped a sponge into my paint and dotted the paper. "See how much easier that is?"

"Yeah," I replied.

"Hey, Gina, can I see something?" Kevin smiled at me with his boyish charm.

"Ok," I blushed, and I passed him my canvas.

"No, not your painting," Kevin said and he pulled my sunglasses away from my face. "Just what I thought."

"What?" I panicked. Oh no, this is where he found out the truth and went running through the forest back to the campsite.

"You have pretty eyes," Kevin stated.

I blushed and looked back to my painting. What was wrong with this boy? Couldn't he see I was ugly? I was beginning to think that he was a blind painter like Stevie Wonder was a blind musician. There was definitely something wrong with him if he thought I was pretty.

"I have to go," I started to pack up my paints. I threw out the stained water in my cup and washed my brushes off in the river.

"Hey, wait!" Kevin called out to me. "I never got to see your painting."

Quickly I handed my picture over to him to critique.

"You have a true sense of expression here. Definite sense of boldness in color and brush strokes," Kevin spoke of my work.

"So who am I like?"

"You remind me of this one artist. She's a great painter, even if she's a little shy about showing her work."

"Who?"

"Her name is Gina. She wears big sunglasses to hide her face, and a silly hat to hide her hair, yet she doesn't need to hide. I look at your painting, Gina, and I see a girl who wants to be seen. So do yourself a favor in life and be seen, don't hide."

"I don't …," I quivered.

"Gina, do you have a family that supports you in your talent?" Kevin frowned at me.

I looked back in the general direction of my family. I hated to admit the truth because it just made me lonelier. I didn't want to say it, because it always made me cry.

"No," I tried to hide my face.

"That's too bad. You're going to have a hard time of it in life," said Kevin.

I didn't want to hear anymore. I couldn't bear it. I scooped up my paint box and stood up.

"Gina, before you take off I want to tell you something. People are always going to look at you as if you're different because you can do something they can't do. I want to tell you that you're not different, you are the same as every artist I have ever met. We are a special breed of people who can see life, and live it, and crawl around inside of it, and come to terms with it. There are more people like us than you think. You're not a freak, Gina, you are someone special with a special gift."

I nodded my head and wiped away the stray tears that rolled across my cheek. He had understood me and filled a part of me that felt empty. I didn't want it to end, I wanted to ride off with this boy and be with people like myself. I didn't want to hide any more.

"Bye, Kevin," I gave him a quick hug.

"Bye, Gina. Take care of yourself," he nodded.

I wandered back to camp in quiet thought. My parents were good, loving people but they never listened to me. Whenever I tried to talk to let them know the woman I was becoming it somehow came out I was being demanding. So I never spoke. I became invisible. I closed out my family and hid in my room, sheltered in a world I created for myself. I painted a picture of bright-colored flowers, blue skies, fluffy white clouds, and a valley below and I put myself in it. Kevin was right, it was difficult being the creative one in a noncreative family. I can hear each individual note in a choir, I can feel a painting, I can see the inside of a drop of rain, and I understood the meaning of words that were spoken from the hearts of man. I was alone in this world with parents who talked of cattle prices and grain shares, a sister who noticed no one but herself, and a little brother who thought the world of Tonka cars.

My hero when I was young was my cousin Mervin. When I think back on it, we must have seemed like such an odd pair. Mervin was seven years older than I. I was such a baby when Mervin was already in college. I was barely five feet tall, and Mervin was already six feet. How I adored him though, with his dark brown eyes and curly brown hair.

Mervin was like fresh rain on a summer morning, he made all the flowers bloom around me, and more importantly he loved me like a little sister. I did have my problems with Mervin, the greatest being that I only saw him at Christmas at the family party. One Christmas sticks out more than all the others.

"So what is the matter?", Mervin smiled at me.

"My dad", I spoke softly, "He wants me to go to university and be a teacher or something"

"Do you want to do that?"

"No", I almost wept, "I want to be an artist. I want to sing and dance"

"Then that is what you should do", Mervin smiled at me, "You should never be anyone but yourself"

Mervin was right. I needed to be myself, but how do you make my family understand that?

I wish with all my heart I could have Mervin around with me always. He always knew the right thing to say. He always made me feel good about being me. He always made me feel precious. He still does.

By the time I got back to camp, I had asked myself the hardest question that we all as men and as women ask of ourselves, "Where do I belong in this world?" I grabbed my suitcase out of the trunk of the car and stepped into the tent trailer and sighed. There were no answers, just more questions.

In the morning we headed up to Grande Prairie and then to Peace River. The next day we were off to Lesser Slave Lake, the largest lake in Alberta. Slowly we winded our way back home, ending another summer vacation.

The next summer Patty would leave home and go to college. As Mom and I packed up Patty's room, I came across her uncompleted tour book. I opened the book and flipped through all the pages. It felt sad somehow, like it knew it was never going to be finished.

Children have this awful habit of growing up and wanting to start their own lives, and you can't stop it. I wanted to stop Patty. I didn't want our family to change. I didn't want to be a family member short. I wanted my sister. I closed the tour book and put it inside my mom's memory box. I felt it shouldn't go with Patty, it should stay with my parents. It was a reminder of our last family vacation as a party of five.

I decided there that change can be good, and change can be bad. I really hated the bad.

CHAPTER FIVE

1985: MOTELS AND DRIVER'S LICENSES

Yep, everything had changed. 1985 was the year I graduated from high school and my parents decided to go to a motel. I couldn't believe it! The man who always had to do everything the cheap way, the bargain hunter, the clearance sale guy was going to book a motel for our holidays. Heck, even buying groceries with Dad was an experience.

"All we need is a 2L of milk, Dad," I would pick a small carton and put in the basket. "There's not much room in the cooler."

"Now hold on there. Look at the amount you pay in a 2L. Consider the amount in a 2L carton, now look at the 4L. It's only seventy-five cents more and you get an extra 2L of milk. So it's a better buy if you buy the 4L," Dad would lecture.

"Yes, Dad. I understand, it's a better deal but we don't need all that milk. We don't have room in the cooler and we couldn't possibly drink all that milk before it spoils," I said.

"Well, maybe you have money to waste, kid, but I don't. When you grow up you can buy your 2L of milk and waste your own money," said Dad as he lifted the 4L carton of milk into his cart.

"What's next on the list?" Dad asked.

"Cereal," I said as Dad and I would walk over to the breakfast food aisle. "Here's Honeycomb, Dad, you like that one."

"Not that one, Gina. Look at the amount of grams you get per box, now look at the price of that one per box. You get a better deal if you buy that family size one, because it's a difference of only $1.25."

"I know, Dad, but we don't need all this food. We are travelling for only six days, not six weeks," I said, exasperated.

"Look, kid, it's my money and my cereal. I'm buying it and that's final," Dad would say sternly.

This type of shopping went on for hours over everything in the store from bread to bacon. Now you understand what I meant that I couldn't believe my dad is spending money on a motel.

"I can't believe it!" I told my mom as she was packing her suitcase. "Dad does know he has to pay money for a room, right?"

"Yes, Gina," Mom shook her head at me.

"I just can't believe we're not camping," I said.

"Well, it's just that your father and I felt that the tent trailer is a lot of work for just four people," Mom looked up at me and smiled. "Don't worry, honey, we'll still have fun."

Mom didn't know it then, but she was so right. It was probably the best summer holiday we ever had.

Camping in a motel is so much different than camping in general. For one, all the pots and pans stay home. Even the way you pack your suitcase is different. When camping in a campsite, you pack sensibly. Sensible walking shoes, sensible clothes, sensible coats, and sensible accessories. When you camp in a motel, it becomes a question of fashion. What looks good, what flatters your body type, what is the right color, and do you have a purse, shoes, and sunglasses to match it all. It would be the first time I ever packed a dress. I don't remember wearing it but I had it all the same.

Mom (a smart lady) went to AMA and picked up a motel registration book. It was amazing to look at. It had listings on every motel, hotel, inn, campsite, and hostel across Canada. It also included prices, amenities, phone numbers, fax numbers, and all the extras. Everything you wanted to know before you got there.

Mom and Dad planned a vacation this year to go to Radium Hot Springs and then a few days at Golden, BC.

My mom (again, I'll say she is the smartest woman in the

world) looked up a nice place to stay at Radium, called Spur Valley Resort. This place had everything! Spur Valley is located approximately twenty-six kilometers north of Inverness. A small sign off the side of the highway points the way to a paradise in the valley. Surrounded by cliffs, trees, and a fast rushing creek, a tennis court, a clubhouse with a grocery store below, a playground, a campsite area, RV parking, public washroom/shower/laundry facilities, cabins, and best of all a pool, all for the low cost of forty dollars a night.

With luggage in tow we checked into the cutest little cabin I had ever seen in my life. Cedar walls throughout, with area rugs on the floor, it had a master bedroom with a dresser and a second bedroom with bunk beds and a dresser. It had a mini stove, mini fridge, sink, and cabinets. There was a small bathroom with sink, shower, and toilet. A small living room with a couch (that flips into another bed), a TV, radio, coffee table, and lamps. In the kitchen there was a table set for four people, and all the accessories that one requires in a kitchen like pots and pans, utensils, spatulas, toaster, coffee pot, tea pot, and tea towels. It was adorable.

For me, the best part of that cabin was the fast rushing creek that flowed only ten feet from the back door. The water was only five or six feet deep and icy cold, and it rushed like a river. I loved it. I spent the entire two days with my window open just so I could hear that water.

Jamie and I ran into the cabin and quickly unpacked. It was time to explore. We found hiking trails that led up into the cliffs, a full tennis court, and friendly kids who were looking for new friends.

"Come on, we're going to the hot springs," said Dad. He caught us chatting with new kids by the washrooms.

"No, Dad. We're having fun!" Jamie answered.

"Look, kid, I didn't bring you here to have fun. You can go home and have fun. Now come on, we're going to the hot springs," Dad grunted at us and walked back to the cabin.

Jamie and I looked at each other with a puzzled look on our faces. He didn't bring us here to have fun? Have fun at home? Weren't holidays about having fun NOT at home? No matter. Jamie and I just shook our heads and followed Dad to the car.

Dad grumbled all the way to the pool. The only time his face lit up was when he saw some mountain goats standing by the side of the road.

"Hey, how about we pull over and feed the goats," Dad called back to us.

"Swell," Jamie and I answered. We fed goats a hundred times; it was no big deal to us anymore.

"Come on, it'll be fun," Dad said as he pulled over the car.

The goats right away came up to the car looking for handouts. The big-horn sheep is the common name for this animal that resembles the common variety goat. Three times the size with large horns, they are most famous for the clashing of horns that can be heard for miles when the males rival for the females. Nowadays, it is illegal to stop by the road and feed these animals due to the high volumes of deaths that occur by passing traffic.

Not that it would ever stop Dad.

"I think I have a loaf of bread in here someplace," said Mom. Jamie and I just sat there as Mom looked in the grocery bag beside her in the front seat. "Maybe I'll just give them leftover sandwiches from lunch"

"I doubt if the goat wants a hamburger with cheese," I sulked.

"It's a goat. It'll eat anything, including the car," replied Dad.

Dad found a sandwich and opened the car door. (Now for any goat-feeders out there, I have some advice for you: DON'T OPEN YOUR DOOR!) Too late; Dad opened the door and in came one hoof and a fuzzy muzzle. The goat took the bite-size piece of food and gulped it down and was looking for more. Mom ripped off another piece of the sandwich, and while she was busy ripping bread and hamburger pieces, in came another hoof. Quickly we gave the goat what he was looking for, but like all goats he was greedy and came looking for more. Mom let out a frazzled gasp and reached into her grocery bag.

It was around this point that the goat must have thought she was too slow and went to look for the sandwich himself. The next thing we knew the entire body of the goat was in the car.

"Gene, get him out of here!" Mom yelled and gave the goat a shove. "Don't worry," said Dad. He ran around to Mom's side of the car and opened the door, hoping that the goat would just pass through the other side. Well, all this did was open up another portal for another goat to get in. Within a few minutes we had two goats in the car.

"Gene!" Mom yelled. "Get them out of here!"

Jamie and I sat in the back and laughed at the goat trying to nibble Mom's hair. Dad reached into the front seat and grabbed the food bag and threw the bread into the ditch. Thankfully the goats walked through the other side and fell for the bait. With both goats now back in the ditch, Mom and Dad quickly closed their car doors and bolted for the highway as if we robbed a bank.

"Well, that was an experience," said Mom. She kept wiping the goat fur off her clothes with her fingers as we made our way to the pool.

Indeed it was an experience. I'll never forget those goats getting behind the wheel, looking around as if they wanted a map. Bleating away to tell their friends, "Hey, get in! Yeah, the old guy fell for it. We got the women and cold sandwiches. We can make Vegas by morning!"

Determined, Dad pressed on to the pool. On the walls of the reception area there was a mural of the history of the pool's origins. I studied the brightly colored murals with fascination. On the first panel it showed the native people sitting in the primitive pool of hot water. Then in another panel it showed the British and the French, who colonized the area and took it all away from the native people (hmm, what else it new?). Today it is a modernized outdoor hot pool, with a cold pool and water slides. I rested along the edges of the pool admiring all the boys through my sunglasses, and there were a lot of boys to admire.

Other than the boys the highlight of my visit was the ten Swedish and Finnish women who were standing buck-naked behind a small wall slapping themselves until they were as red as a lobster.

"It is to improve circulation," one woman told my mother and I through a strained accent.

"Oh," we blushed and quickly moved on to the changing rooms.

I have no problem with the naked body, unless it's unexpected. Ten naked women who only stood behind a small partition that anyone could come around was somewhat of a shock to us. In Canada women are taught to be a little more demure with our bodies, we are not that bold.

Dressed and still smelling of the pool, we made our way out to the car.

There is a time when all fathers and sons learn and share from one another. It is a time that replaces all other memories. It holds fast in your heart that you carry into your old age. For Jamie this time came when he learnt to drive the car.

"Dad, can I drive?" asked a timid Jamie.

"You? You?" a frazzled Dad answered. "You can't drive!"

"Yes, I can. I got my learner's permit," Jamie announced proudly.

"Fine. Fine," grumped Dad. "But I get to sit up front with you."

Jamie buckled himself into the front seat and carefully pulled out of the parking lot. Jamie's driving became the sole amusement for Mother and I. For Jamie and Dad it became something much more. It was a small fragment of time when they were just a boy and his dad, a moment they'll always have. (But then maybe Jamie doesn't want to.)

"Jamie, you're going too fast. Slow down," Dad gave the order.

Jamie responded as a good son should and slowed the car down.

"Jamie, why are you going so slow?" questioned Dad a few minutes later.

"You told me to," Jamie answered.

"No, I didn't."

"Yes, you did."

Jamie was a good son and wanted to impress Dad with his driving skills more than anything. So as a kid trying to impress his father would do, Jamie applied the gas and sped up the car.

One thing about mountain driving is that it is not an ordinary stretch of road. There are twists, sharp turns, sharp inclines, and sharp drops. For a fourteen-year-old driver who was just learning to drive, I thought Jamie was an excellent driver. He was doing wonderfully well. (Today he's a picker truck operator for the oil industry.) It is easy to become blinded in the mountains by heavy fog, heavy rain, trees, rocks, cliffs, goats, deer, elk, and moose. (In Jamie's case, it was just as easy to become blinded by girls.)

"JAMIE!!!!!! STOP!!!!!" Dad yelled.

Without a moment's hesitation Jamie came to a full and sudden stop by screeching the brakes.

"What the hell's the matter with you, kid?!!! Didn't you see those mountain goats?!!" Dad yelled.

"No, I didn't," Jamie answered quietly and put his head on the steering wheel.

"What the heck were you looking at, kid?" Dad lectured.

"I'm sorry, Dad." Jamie thought for moment and then smiled. "I was looking at that girl over there."

"A girl?!! A girl?!!" Dad sputtered. His face was turning red. "You wouldn't know what to do with a girl if you had one."

"Sure, I would, Dad," Jamie smiled from ear to ear and sang, "I'd lay her downnnnn …."

"Jane, Jane! Did you just hear what our son said?" Dad's face was now turning purple. Any more shocks about Jamie's libido and Dad was going to have a stroke.

Mom and I couldn't answer because we were laughing too hard. Father's face was about to burst with contempt for the whole situation but what we found funny was that if any girl had strolled up to Jamie he probably would've wet himself.

On the ride back to the cabin, I looked out my car window but I didn't see anything. My mind raced with thoughts of Jamie. He was no longer the cute little blond baby with the ducky curls on his neck. The rosy cheeks and gentle smile all were faded now as he was becoming a young man. Gone was his love for Tonka cars, and plastic army men; now his mind was filled with girls.

I still thought of Jamie as my sweet, innocent little brother. Jamie, my charmer. Jamie, the boy who tried to defy gravity and drive his plastic pedal tractor up the side of the basement wall. Now he was a young man; the child I loved was gone forever.

My heart broke. Patty was gone to college and had fallen in love. She was set to marry soon. I graduated and was being sent to college. Only Jamie was left at home. Everything was changing again, and not for the better. I suddenly felt overwhelmed with sadness. I loved my family and I wanted us all to stay together. If only the car was a time machine, I'd tell Dad to go back and leave us there.

That night I tried to let the creek lull me to sleep. It didn't, nor did the wind blowing through the trees. No matter how hard I tried, I couldn't shake the feeling that I was losing my family and this was probably the last time I would ever travel with Jamie ever again.

I didn't want the change to come, but I couldn't stop it. I closed my eyes with my final thoughts being that I was going to make the best of this holiday because you can't stop people from growing up, and you can't stop people from leaving. Since you can't change anything, you might as well enjoy what time you have left, and I did.

In the morning, the whole family awoke to the sun and another day. The two days had passed by so fast and here we were already packing the car and moving on to the town of Golden.

Jamie and I sat on the front porch watching Mom and Dad pack up our luggage and clean up the cabin. Jamie sighed and looked forlornly at the car.

"So I hear you're mad at me," Dad sat down beside Jamie.

"No. I'm not."

"Yes, you are."

"No, I'm not," Jamie said in a more direct voice.

"Yes, you are because I made problems for you when you were driving yesterday," said Dad.

"No. Really, I'm not mad."

"Yes, you are. Just admit it! Just admit it! Admit it! Admit it!" Dad taunted.

"Fine!" Jamie yelled. "I'm mad at you!" Jamie's hands balled into fists. "Is that what you want to hear, Dad?"

"Yes, it is," Dad smiled and threw the car keys at Jamie. "Now shut up and drive."

Jamie frowned as he looked down at the keys in his hand. He opened his mouth as if he was going to say something but instead he shook his head and opened the car door and got in.

Us kids have known from experience that Dad never says he's sorry, because to Dad, he never makes mistakes. How can he? He's a genius. Or at least that's what he always tried to tell us kids. Dad even invented his own nickname, "Eugenius" — "You-gene-ius." Yeah, he thought that was quite clever. However, as a genius, Dad's rational reasoning left something to be desired. Just as his conversations with his son didn't always make sense. Five minutes down the road they were at it again.

"I said, slow down, kid. You're going too fast," said Dad as he glanced at the speedometer.

"I am not!" Jamie challenged. "I'm doing the speed limit."

"Well, it's too fast."

"How can the speed limit be too fast when it's the speed limit?" questioned Jamie.

"Don't ask questions, just concentrate on the road," Dad pointed in front of himself to the road ahead.

"I am!" shouted Jamie.

"You are not!" Dad shouted back.

For a moment there was utter silence in the car. No one dared to speak (heck, no one dared to breathe). Dad leaned over and looked at the speedometer again.

"Slow down, you're going too fast."

"I am not!" Jamie growled. "I told you, I am going the speed limit."

Fearing another fight, Dad decided to end it — with us girls.

"Girls. Girls. Did I say anything about the boy going too slow?" Dad turned around and faced Mom and I.

Now Mom and I are not stupid. We knew we couldn't choose a side. If we supported Dad it could hurt a very tender young driver. If we supported Jamie we could hurt Dad. There were no winners, only losers. We opted out for a side door, an exit, an escape hatch. We couldn't be judges; it would be suicide. So I decided to lead the way out of the verbal battle, with an ordinary looking tree by the side of the road.

"Oh, Mom. Look at that tree!" I pointed out.

"Oh, yes," Mom responded. "Isn't it amazing?"

Dad grunted as he turned back to the face the road.

"It's useless getting anything out of those two," Dad snorted.

So we traveled down the highway once more. For the moment Jamie's driving skills were all but forgotten as the two men talked about the lack of integrity in women and their inability to give an honest answer to a simple question.

"And that is why women will never become prime ministers," Dad ended the conversation.

"I know," Jamie agreed.

Mom and I didn't say anything. We just smiled and laid back and enjoyed the ride.

CHAPTER SIX

LITTLE RED CANOES

It was a long ride to Golden and it was time for lunch. My dad (alias: the Poodle, alias: El Cheapo) decided that Emerald Lake was a lovely place to rest for lunch. Mom and I grew excited as we pulled up towards a gorgeous timber hotel. It looked so fancy and decadent; our taste buds were watering. We pointed out to my brother all the empty parking lots (which he kept missing), and sank back in our seats with utter disappointment. It came as no surprise to us when he drove right past the hotel and parked at a picnic table by the lake.

Jamie, Mom, and I all sighed as Dad threw cold roast beef sandwiches on the table in front of us. I don't know if I can express the exhilaration that a beef farming family can feel to have more beef on their summer holidays. I would look pensively at the neighbor's picnic of fried chicken and potato salad with dinner rolls and strawberries. I had to look away, it was too much.

"I'm sorry," Jamie would apologize for the second time as we bit into the sandwiches. "Dad made me."

"It's ok," we told him. Mom and I certainly knew how Dad was. Dad was the sort of person who would buy three watermelons on sale in the grocery store and make you eat all the melons before they went bad, in one day, because he couldn't fit them in the car trunk.

Sometimes it seems that all logic leaves Dad's head when he's on holiday. I remember when I was thirteen and we were on one of our many trips to the mountains. Dad wanted water in the water jug, so Mom grabbed a jug and found the pump and began to fill it.

"Hold it still!" growled Dad.

"I am!" shouted Mom. Water splashed all over the sides as she struggled to hold the heavy jug.

"Oh, give me that!" grouched Dad. Not realizing the pump handle swung 360 degrees around, Dad pushed it away and it hit Mom right on the edge of her right eye.

"Aaaaaaah!" screamed Mom as she crawled on the ground, holding her eye.

Us kids came running over as Mom's screaming got louder and louder. It occurred to us that Mom may have lost her eye, and we would have to volunteer to search for it. Of course all we had to do was look for the bloody trail, but how hard could that be?

Fortunately, the eye was still in the socket but the end result was a swollen, bruised eye. In fact, it was so badly swollen, it had closed her eye completely shut. My poor mother had to put up with five days of black eye and migraine headaches. In retrospect Mom probably had a concussion, but Dad was on holiday, and when my father was on holiday, he never touched civilization.

So if you were attacked by ravenous beavers and you had your arm bitten off, too bad! Or if killer Canadian geese pecked off your legs, no use crying! Dad was on holiday, and he never heard of the word "hospital." So you better pack up your arms and legs in a cooler, lock them in the trunk of the car until you get back home. Yep, you just better stop the bleeding with a sleeping bag and hope for the best. Do whatever you have to do to survive, because there was no way you were going to be surrounded by doctors and nurses while Dad was enjoying his holiday.

Like I said, all logic leaves Dad when he leaves the farm and sleeps in a tent.

The roast beef sandwiches were mediocre at best, but there was no choice but to eat them or starve. Dad was not into negotiations or food stands.

After lunch we walked around for a few moments just enjoying the serenity and calmness of the lake. There was hardly a soul around; the silence just seemed to make the place even more lovely. Dad, of course, had to shatter it by renting a canoe.

Mom frowned and shook her head at Dad's invitation to tour the lake (she still wasn't friends with water). Then the offer came to me. I was so excited. I looked across the lake to the shore at the other side; a sense of adventure swept over me. I held my breath as I took a step forward, but sealed my fate when I looked back at Mom. She had a sad "don't leave me" smile on her face. I couldn't do it. I waved Dad off and stepped back to be with Mom. The offer was then passed to Jamie and he accepted. I watched Jamie climb into the boat and together a father and son glided across the silent water as if they there were two loons, with the etches of waves that flowed silently behind them. How peaceful, how tranquil, what bliss was this rapture, and then a string of verbal anger echoed across the lake from the direction of Dad and Jamie and the little red canoe.

"Jamie, paddle on the other side. I'm left, and you're right!" shouted Dad.

"No, I'm the lead. You paddle right and I'm left," Jamie shouted back.

"Look, kid, I said put your paddle on the other side."

"No, you put YOUR paddle on the other side!"

This seemed awfully familiar to Mom and I, who had been putting up with the battle of wills in the car for hours, so we did the most sensible thing a woman can do when the men in her life are fighting: We walked away and pretended we didn't know them. As we walked, the canoe drifted in circles as Dad and Jamie paddled on the same side of the canoe. Slowly the canoe edged toward a white bridge; the whole time the pair were arguing as to who put the paddle on which side of the canoe.

Finally a man came on to the bridge. He stood for a moment as if in pensive thought and frowned at the canoe circling towards him. Hearing the string of yelling coming the red canoe's directions, the man finally put an end to it. "Hey, you two! You paddle on the left side, and you paddle on the right!"

Dad and Jamie looked at each other in shock. I don't think it ever occurred to them that other people could overhear the shouting. Suddenly the argument over whose paddle goes where was over as Dad and Jamie glided across the water. Mom and I watched the father and son team until they were out of sight.

The crisis over the paddle in the water argument had appeared to be solved and us women were now on our own to explore the park. We gushed over the tall green pine trees, the emerald green of the lake, the blue sky, and the squirrels that chattered happily to us as we passed them. We decided to follow the path that led up to the hotel. We admired the timber logs that framed the building and peered into the windows of the restaurant. It was charming with dusty rose tablecloths, a stone fireplace that seemed to go through a vaulted ceiling, and timber wood tables. Upstairs rooms were available for a hefty price, with balconies that hung right over the water.

I felt my imagination drifting away again. I was enchanted with the man of dreams. We would sit at the little wooden table by the fireplace and drink champagne. Laughing and blushing the way lovers do, we would eventually find our way to our room. I imagined we would step out to the balcony and stare in wonder at the lake, which would become black with the blanket of night, a dark abyss with floating stars. Looking up into the night sky we would kiss, as we marveled in the infinite universe. In the morning we would lay in bed with our breakfast and laugh as we fed each other strawberries. Slowly we would make our way out of bed and step out to the balcony and dive into the lake water, and enjoy the cool wetness as it encircled our bodies.

"I want to go over here," said Mom, as she pulled my arm and broke me out of my trance.

Mom and I then wandered over to a group of small cabins and a playground. Satisfied that our curiosity was met, we walked back to the picnic table and waited for the men. Jamie was the first to come ashore and sit by us girls.

"Where's your father?" asked Mom.

"Taking back the canoe," said Jamie.

Silence.

"Was it nice out there?" I asked.

"Yeah," shrugged Jamie.

Again, silence.

"Hit any trouble spots?" I asked. I was trying my best to have a conversation.

"Nope," Jamie shrugged. Again silence. It would seem that there was nothing more to say. "Dad had to take a shit," Jamie smiled up at me.

JACKPOT!!!! It was not often you got anything on Dad because he always said he was perfect (all geniuses are), but knowing Dad had to dip his torso in the bush was too good to be true.

"Are you sure?" I smiled at Jamie.

"Yep, he did it," Jamie smiled back.

This information was pure gold, baby! Jamie and I just smiled at each other, a silent respect for the intelligence received.

No one said a word as we piled back into the car. Finally when Dad sat down and made his way out on the highway again, I leaned forward in my seat and threaded my fingers through Dad's hair. It felt soft and fine, like a child's.

"So, Dad," I whispered in my most affectionate voice. "Does grass stick to your ass?"

"Oh, oh, oh, oh," Dad sputtered, his face turning almost purple. "That kid! Can't tell you we had a good time. No, no, the kid had to tell you that Dad had to take a shit!"

Dad may have said more at this point, but we were all laughing too hard to hear what he was saying. It would be a few more hours until we calmed down again and enjoyed the rest of the trip to Golden.

CHAPTER SEVEN

TRAINS AND THE SUNNY BROOK MOTEL

It was after supper when we arrived in Golden, BC. Golden is a lovely little city built into two levels; that is, the city is sprawled across the hillside and into the valley below. We admired the long train of over 110 cars, as it blew its whistle signaling to the valley below its arrival. The hills, covered in a pine forest, seemed to cuddle the green valley floor below. Golden was indeed, well … Golden.

Dad decided that Mom (a mere woman) was not going to have the title of "Best Hotel Picker," so we all waited patiently as Dad thumbed through the AMA book that we all referred to now as the "Vacation Bible." Smiling, Dad announced that he had found one, a lovely little motel called … The Sunny Brook Motel.

"Doesn't that sound nice?" said Dad as he stopped at a gas station to make the reservations.

When we arrived we found a clean, neat motel for fifty dollars a night that included a kitchenette, a double bed and two singles, and a little table and chairs. Of course it had gone completely unnoticed to us that the motel was deserted, but we just figured that we were the first to arrive and claim this rare gem. Other people would show up later.

Dad bragged about how he found the deal of the century and how he had one up on Mom. Us kids decided to explore our new environment. I imagined that Jamie and I were explorers, sent to find a rare treasure, "The lost brook of the Sunny Brook Motel." About ten feet from the motel, Jamie and I found a dried-up creek bed. We sat down and studied the dried green algae.

"Could this be possible?" I asked Jamie. "Has the Sunny Brook become … Sunny Dried?"

On the other side of the trees is a train track and some equipment left by the CN train crew. I know. I know. You're probably thinking we should've said something to our parents, but we were kids; who thinks of these things? It never seemed important at the time.

After we ate our supper in the motel, we settled in with our luggage for the night. (I want to mention here and now that the events that occurred that night did happen over twenty years ago. Also it has no bearing on the motel; it's not their fault that a train runs past their back door.) As I said, we settled in for the night, and at four o'clock in the morning it began.

I woke up, my heart pounding in my chest. White lights flashed around the room, the room rumbled as if we were caught inside the spin cycle of a washing machine. Pictures knocked against the wall, my lamp fell on the floor. I screamed only for my voice to be lost in the deafening noise.

"What's going on?!" I yelled. I was frightened. I had seen movies of alien invasions and I was pretty sure I was caught up in one. I screamed again, and saw my mom crossing the room in her white nightgown against the flashes of white light.

"It's ok!" Mom shouted. "It's just a train passing by!" She picked up my lamp and placed it on my table, only to have it fall off again.

Jamie rolled around in his bed; in his sleep he yelled, "You'll never take me alive!"

Mom and I looked at each other with raised eyebrows.

"Must be some dream!" Mom screamed.

My brother was always an incredible sleeper. Jamie could sleep through planes, trains, and traffic horns but even this was too much as Jamie rolled out of bed and found his family all huddled in the living room. Honestly, it never occurred to any of us that the train tracks we saw everywhere, all over town, would actually have trains on them. As soon as one left, another came barreling down the tracks, whistle blowing, the clanking of metal rims on the rails.

The only other patrons sharing the hotel with us were a young couple. At five o'clock in the morning they had enough. Red eyed from the lack of sleep, they threw their luggage into the back of their car and left. I plugged my ears with my fingers and wished I could go with them.

"It'll pass in a few minutes," Dad yelled to us, and as usual Eugenius was right, for 180 minutes later the trains did finish passing. Right after that we also left with our eyes red, our ears still ringing from the train whistles, and our bodies drained from last night's adventure.

We settled into the car and made our way up the hillside that led out of Golden. Everyone silent from the lack of sleep, Dad turned on the car radio to make noise and to probably keep himself awake.

"Stay in the fabulous HILLSIDE HOTEL!!" the man on the radio announced. "We have waterslides, a pool, and complementary breakfast. Enjoy a candlelit supper by the stone fireplace. A night for four people is only FORTY DOLLARS!!! That's right, only FORTY DOLLARS!!"

Jamie and I squinted at Dad. Not only had he over paid by TEN BUCKS but he robbed us of sleep and waterslides. My God, WATERSLIDES! I could've been basking around a tiled pool looking for men and instead I thought I was in a remake of the classic film, "Close Encounters of the Third Kind."

Jamie reached into the front seat and took the AMA book off the dash and placed it into Mom's hands. "Don't let this book out of your sight," he told her and sat back in his seat again.

It was then that Mom was given the sole responsibility and title of "Hotel Picker." Her pick of the Spur Valley Hotel was a gem of a find. Her title was well earned and respected. Twenty years later, the title is still hers to this very day.

CHAPTER EIGHT

1986: WHERE'S THE GOLD, BOB?

It was my last summer vacation with my family. Although it wasn't spoken, I still knew that, and knowing this gave me considerable sadness. That and the fact that I spent my last year in Edmonton, going to college to become a legal secretary left me confused.

My parents packed up my room with me sobbing and hanging on their legs not to send me, got me an apartment in the city, and sent me to college to take a course I wasn't made for. I was scared to death. I didn't know how to take a bus, pay my bills, or phone for pizza. I don't blame my parents, they were only looking out for me and I appreciated everything they did, but I was too young and not ready.

After working a few weeks for some lawyers, I knew it was not the job for me and I took the summer off and ended up going home to find myself. I was still wandering around the yard asking myself the same questions: "Who am I?" "Why am I here?" "What should I do with my life?" I guess Mom and Dad had enough of me making tracks in the lawn so when they decided to take a family holiday, they asked me to go with them (Jamie stayed home). I accepted the invitation before I took a job as a waitress. I wasn't looking forward to working for a roadside diner but I needed money to take care of myself and time to figure out what I really wanted.

"So where are we going?" I asked as I packed my suitcase.

"To see your uncle and aunt in Barkerville, BC. They have a gold claim there. You can come back home at the end of the week with your aunt and start your new job and your father and I are going to follow your uncle to Norman Wells, Yukon, where he has another gold claim," Mom explained to me.

(Well, it wasn't the sunny beaches of Mexico, but it could still be fun.)

For this adventure my father bought a 1972 camper that slept four. We had a sink, stove, fridge, and a mini closet. Our table turned into a double bed and my parents took the bunk over the truck cab. I personally always thought it depressing with its dark wood interior and old checkered cloth curtains; however, it kept the rain off my head. There's not much more you can ask from a holiday unit than that. In fact the only downfall of a camper is backing it up over the truck bed and hitching it to the truck box. You have to be precise in backing it up and sliding under the camper or else you'll hit the legs and down goes the camper. Once it's on, though, it's like a turtle with a shell.

Barkerville was not an alluring adventure. It wasn't like the time the bear walked through our campsite and missed Dad because he was dressed in a green shirt and brown pants and blended with the trees. This adventure didn't stop at all the BC fruit stands where my dad would pick up ten-pound bags of cherries, peaches, and plums. Dad would pay the fruit vendor the money and mutter under his breath they were all robbers. In the car Dad would share with us kids a peach, a plum, and ten cherries and eat the rest of the fruit himself. He'd drive happily down the road chewing the fruit and spitting cherry pits out the window; when we'd stop for gas the car would be decorated with cherry pits where they were blown in the wind. Honest it looked like we ran down the fruit stand; at least the bees loved us.

No, Barkerville was a different adventure, different in the sense that it was boring. It was dusty, dirty, and muddy in places. You couldn't explore because of the high traffic of bears in the area. There was no forest, no trails, barely a gravel road, and no bathrooms, but the worst of it all: there were no boys!!!!! In fact there was no one for me to talk to. I was the only kid there. Once we ate in my aunt's camper and once they ate in ours. My mom spent her time reading a book, and I spent my time wishing I had a book to read.

One memory stands out on this trip. My uncle was busy showing my dad his fancy new machine that he paid an extraordinary amount of money for to search for gold. He pointed out the dust and dirt it left in a pile behind the machine. He explained the way it works, and the successes he had.

"Ah, I bet I can find gold the old-fashioned way, by panning for it," said Dad.

"Go ahead, help yourself," my uncle smirked. "There's some pans over there, but I'll tell you its no match for my machine."

My dad picked up the little green plastic pan and knelt down by the river and swooshed for the gold. The water circled around and around in the pan; each time my father would let a little of the water and mud drop back into the river until he was left with a fine sediment on the bottom. He repeated this process several times, until finally he jumped up and faced us.

"Look! I found one!" Dad yelled.

My uncle and I came running over to see the small gold nugget roughly the size of a pea that my father had found. I tried to hide my laughter. My uncle and his gold machine turned up empty, while my dad took fifteen minutes out his time and found gold with an ordinary plastic pan. I have to give my uncle credit, though; his machine did make an impressive dust pile that I am sure would be envied by all other dust piles. In fact if there were a dust pile contest, my uncle would be crowned king, because that was some fancy dust if I ever saw some.

I even thought about suggesting he get some security for his dust; it would be a pity if anyone were to steal it.

My father proudly handed over the gold nugget to my uncle and exclaimed, "Maybe you should keep it and figure out what gold looks like." Right after that my dad sat down and panned a few more minutes and found some more gold. This time he kept it.

"As a triumph, man over machine," he told me as he placed the nuggets in a tiny glass vial and put it in the camper.

Thankfully my uncle and my dad had a good relationship, full of a lot of teasing, which neither of them seemed to mind.

Once for a break we all packed up for the day and went into Barkerville. In the early 1800s when the west was discovered to hold gold, the people colonized a town to give supplies to the settlers. It was a cultural mix of people from Canada, the Americans, and even the

Chinese. To keep alive the memory of the hardships these people faced, the present people restored Barkerville as a tourist ghost town.

Actors dressed in old-fashioned suits and dresses retell the tales of the people who once lived there, like the Chinese laundryman (and others like him) who had a claim and struck gold. When he died they poured the gold into his coffin with his body and sent it back to China, which is how China got some of the gold used for their temples and statues.

Then there was the bartender who poured out root beer in an old bar and told tales of the gunfights and mysterious murders that occurred while the gold rush was on. Even the ladies with their fancy ruffled dresses talked in the grocery store of the high prices of corn and coffee, a whole two cents for five pounds of coffee. It made you want to laugh, to think of what we pay for coffee now. Suddenly you didn't think it was funny as they talked about miscarriages, because they had no doctor, and the rapes, because they had no sheriff. You stopped laughing after that.

It occurred to me that Barkerville was a town of desperation, despair, and misery. There was so much loss here, and I wondered why on earth would anyone want to keep this sort of memory alive, but I guess that's why they would want to.

We shouldn't forget who we were, where we came from, and the hardship, the struggle, and the blood that was shed for us all to be here. The people who lived here were real, they came against all the odds, and against hope that they would find gold and live a better life. Some made it, some didn't. In life, we are all doing the same. We struggle against the odds that something better would be out there for us; some of us will make it and some will not. Barkerville is not a town set up for the some who made it, but it's a living testimonial to those who didn't.

On the way home we stopped at a hotel that served huge portions of pie. I felt ashamed of myself. I knew my aunt and uncle were doing their best to entertain me, but I just couldn't find the excitement in dust and dirt. The pie was pretty good, though. I ate the whole piece, which was roughly half the pan.

After a few days, my aunt declared she was ready to return

home. I packed up my things and hugged my parents goodbye and wished them well on the rest of their vacation.

I was a little surprised my aunt asked me to drive her little blue car, but I was happy to as I didn't really want to sit for 700 miles just looking out the window at the scenery.

I got to know my aunt that day. She talked about the places she had been, the first teaching job she ever had, how she met my uncle, she even pointed out a spot where she lived by the river in Jasper.

"Did you have a house there?" I asked.

"No, we lived in a tent."

"How long were you there?" I questioned.

"Not long, just a few months until your uncle was finished working in that area," she answered.

"Was it just the two of you?"

"No, I had my girls with me then."

"You mean you had the girls with you? How old were they?"

"Oh, they were three and one years old then, I think. They could've been older than that even. I remember they were small, still in diapers."

"That must have been hard on you. Where did you do the laundry and get the groceries?" I asked.

"Here in town. There was a laundrymat and a store to buy a few things," my aunt replied.

I looked back at my aunt sitting thoughtfully beside me. I realized she had lived the life of the women in Barkerville. She gave up a home and the security of raising her children in a safe place to be with the man she loved. The tent leaked, the children had to be watched constantly, and she was left to do the cooking and the cleaning over a fire, just to be near him as he worked. She was sacrificing her life to make him happy. Years later I wonder why so many women give up the things that make us complete to be with the men we love. We give up our homes, our careers, our security, and our dreams to make the men in our life happy. We sacrifice so much to the extent that we are not really living life, but only half living in the world.

I studied the road ahead of me; my aunt changed for me that day. She no longer was the lady who made cookies and tea whenever I came over. She was a sister, a woman like me who had loved and loved and loved and loved and in the end gave up everything to be with her husband.

Outside of Jasper, my aunt fell asleep. That was another thing I found out about my aunt that day: She can't stay awake in a moving vehicle and she can snore like a bear.

It wasn't until we pulled up towards my house that my aunt finally woke up.

"We're here," I announced, putting the car into park.

"Where are we?" my Aunt replied, still a little dazed.

"Home."

"Already?"

"Yeah, well, miles seem to fly by when you're fast asleep," I teased and grabbed my luggage out of the back of the car.

Inside the house I saw my brother had done some redecorating. The kitchen chairs were in the living room. The sofa was in the hallway, and the kitchen table was spread apart while he waxed his skis on it. Why, you ask, was my brother waxing his skis in the middle of summer? WHO KNOWS! Needless to say the house was straightened out when my aunt and I came through the door.

I watched my aunt drive off in her little blue car up our driveway. I had gained respect for her on that trip home, a deep and profound admiration for all that she had gone through to make a family and provide a happy and safe home for her children to grow up in. She's retired from teaching but still stays involved with children and their education. She has a lovely house, she raised three beautiful children who all became successful in their careers, but still she has made sacrifices to make the man in her life happy. It's that part that will never be fulfilled that makes us women. It's the common bond that women across this earth will all share and understand.

I never got to spend more time with my aunt and uncle, nor did I ever see the gold claims they had. I cherished the time we spent together, like a secret picture that I put away in my memory box for safekeeping. It's with me always.

I started the job as a waitress and a week later my parents arrived home from the Yukon. They told me stories of roads that hugged the cliffs high above the valley below, and rugged men, and huge salmon and riverboats, and incredible scenery.

"Oh, sure, have fun without me," I sulked on Mom's bed.

"Well, next time you can come with us," Mom said and smiled at me.

Life is unpredictable, unexpected, and full of mystery. There is no way you can see the future and know how your life, or anyone else's life, is going to turn out.

Two years later we were told that Dad was diagnosed with mental depression, a genetically inherited chemical imbalance in the brain that leaves you feeling that life is hopeless, you are filled with loss and misery and you don't know why. My dad would spend the rest of his life knowing that his thinking was wrong and he was going to cure it with food.

"This radish is the answer," Dad would declare and eat the whole bowl.

It would then become tomatoes, eggs, cabbage, grapefruit, dandelion leaves, and even stinging nettles. My dad was desperate to become the man he once was, and I was desperate to have the man he once was back.

There are days when my father was full of life and happy. In those brief moments I had my dad back. The man I spent my life getting to know. The man who went to a military air show and sat beside the officers in uniform and complained about the waste of taxpayers' money to fly loops in the sky with a plane. The man who went to Kimberly, BC and rang the town clock so much the businesspeople came out and told him to get away from that clock. The man who bragged about the watermelon he grew only to slice one open and find out it was a small pumpkin. The man who was going to produce a new source of energy by taking the power lines down and using a few pans of water in the garage. The guy who said we should pray for a strange woman's bust line because it must be hard on her back. The man who stayed up until dawn playing cards because he was determined to beat his grandson in a card game. The king of auction sales, with treasures like bicycles with no wheels, locked doorknobs with no keys, and a tent with no poles, bought because it only cost a dollar and it was a good deal. These are only a fleeting memory of the happy times.

Then, there were the sad moments, when Dad closed off the world, as if he were a closing a pair of curtains. Vacations were sullen and sad now. Dad would walk with us on the pier on Vancouver Island and wouldn't utter a word. He would fly home in the plane and not even look out the window. You had no idea if Dad was happy or not. At home he spent hours reading his Bible in his favorite chair, never uttering a word. There were no more hugs and laughter as there had once been. The man who was my dad was gone.

Family vacations were over, and like a book we closed the cover and never looked back.

CHAPTER NINE

1989: CHEESIES AND BLACK BEARS

I raged a war inside of me. Who did I want to please most in this world? My father or myself? It was a tough decision, because I loved my father. He was my king, my leader, and my educator. However, I had to make myself happy and choose a life that I wanted. I decided art would be that life. My choice was a hard concept for my father to accept.

"I just don't understand, kid. Why don't you want to be a nurse? They make good money, you know."

"I can't be a nurse. I faint at the sight of blood. Besides, I am too sensitive. Some little kid might come in hurt and I'd fall apart."

"You'd get over it," Dad tried to assure me.

"Dad, I don't want to be a nurse, ok?"

"Well, how about a teacher? You'd get a good pension and you get two months in the summer off."

"Dad, why can't you just love me as I am? I'm an artist, Dad. I don't want to be a teacher or a nurse. I got a student loan on my own, and this is what I want to do with it."

"Fine, be that way," Dad shrugged me off. "You'll probably starve and die."

When Dad left my room, I sobbed and cried. I was nineteen and all I wanted in the whole world was for my father to love me for the person I was. Four months ago I had enrolled myself in an art college in Dawson Creek, BC, and to my excitement I was accepted.

It would become the most pivotal point in the direction of my life. I sat in the college art room with twenty-four other artists and shared the creative energy that flowed through the room. Still, I felt as though I needed to hold back. I did, until I met Lois Smith. Lois was an elderly lady that I met in my art classes; she was kind and gentle, and always had a smile. It was because of Lois that I also got into the College Choir and local church choir. It was also because of Lois's gentle reassurance that I knew I had a place in this world and that I belonged. I was starting to feel the creative life I craved for.

Amongst my peers I was accepted and even respected for all the many talents that I possessed. Finally after years of searching and doubting, I had found myself. A funny thing happens when you find yourself; people find you too. I started selling my artwork to a local gallery, I was singing in a major choir, and I even did some local acting. That is where I met Wade.

My dorm mother asked me if I would like to do some singing and acting for a local restaurant in town for a Halloween party the restaurant was providing for its employees. I jumped enthusiastically in. I knew my father would have frowned on such behavior from me, but my father wasn't here. I was 500 miles from home, and I was free to be myself. I met my darling, the man who would be my husband, the night before the party. He sat at a video game machine with his large hands wrapped around a pint of beer, his long legs in grey jeans stretched out into the aisle, his broad shoulders in a blue flannel jacket were relaxed and slumped into his chair. Upon his head was curly, red hair and he had a red beard that shone like a new penny. He was the most beautiful boy I had ever seen in my life. To me he was the color of autumn, and the freshness of spring. One glance and I was in love. Problem was he didn't know who I was. I had thought about buying him a beer, but I decided that beautiful boys like that didn't notice girls like me — so I went home.

The next day I went back to the restaurant to set up for my scene in the Halloween party. I was an Irish bride with my throat slashed by a jealous husband who found out I was in love with another man. I was quite a sight with my eyes blacked in, and red paint and gel on my throat. Before I had gone upstairs for the costume change, I saw the red-haired boy at the video machine talking to a boy in my art class. What a stroke of good luck! I went over to say hello to my fellow classmate and gave my brightest smile to the red-haired boy. He didn't even look at me.

"Oh, well," I thought to myself. "You didn't really expect him to notice you, did you?"

I went on with the play that evening, impressing many people who thought I was a professional actress. After the Halloween party there was a dance being held in the hotel next door. I was asked to attend and I accepted. Coming down the stairs, a blond boy ran up to me and said his friend wanted to dance with me. His friend turned out to be my red-haired boy!

"Hi, I'm Wade." He spoke softly. "I'm a chef here."

"I'm Gina," I smiled and I placed my hand in his as he led me out to the dance floor.

We danced all night long that night. In Wade's arms I found out the part in my life I was missing: acceptance for who I was. Wade never once tried to force me into careers I didn't want to be in, nor did he want me to change the dreams I held in my heart. Maybe he didn't understand the passion and fire that runs through me, nor did he see "color" or the ocean in a drop of rain, but Wade saw me. Just Gina. What made it perfect was our first kiss. The world stopped, and music played from somewhere far away. My heart raced, and my skin felt on fire. Wade was my match in life. I knew it from that very first kiss.

Two weeks later we were engaged and nine months later we were married. Life with Wade has been a whirlwind, and it still is today.

Of course while dating, it is important to see if you have the same things in common. No sense agreeing to marry someone if you don't have at least one thing in common. Nope, better make sure he fits the most important parts of your plans.

Cooking? Check!

Dancing? Check!

Cuddling? Check! Check!

Camping? DEFINITELY!

What a stroke of good fortune that I should meet someone

who is an avid fisherman and camper. What pleasure I felt when Wade offered to take me on a real overnight camping trip.

"Do we need a map to get to Moonshine Lake?" I asked as I packed the four-door, Ford Fairmont car.

"No, I know where we're going," Wade stuffed the sleeping bags in the trunk of the car.

"Are you sure you know the way?"

"Look, this is my old stomping grounds," Wade reassured me. "I know this place like the back of my hand."

I relaxed a little. My darling knew what he was doing. I mean, up until now all we had was little day trips, and it didn't always turn out well. Like the time we went fishing and picnicking at Swan Lake.

"Uh, oh," I frowned. "We forgot our frying pan."

"That's ok," Wade smiled. "We'll just use our spatula."

I watched my boyfriend balance a tofu patty on the spatula over a blazing fire. It was going pretty well until it fell off into the fire.

"That'll be mine," said Wade as he fished the patty out of the ashes.

"You bet it is, buddy," I muttered under my breath.

Of course, this adventure was only minor compared to the experience of fishing with Wade at the Kiskatinaw River.

Wade's uncle has a farm that borders on the river, and we decided to wander down to the beach with a picnic basket and our fishing poles for an afternoon of nature.

The river was excellent for pickerel. So we set up our lines and cast them across the swift-flowing water, letting the lines softly drift towards the bottom and reeling them back in again. Over and over we cast and reeled in our lines. Over and over we let them drift to the bottom and brought them back home again. Unfortunately, I let my cast drift too far and sink too low.

"Uh, oh," I grumbled. "I'm stuck." I tugged on the line repeatedly with no success.

"Well, if you think I'm going out there to save you, you can just forget it, missy," Wade said sternly.

"Fine, I'll get it myself."

I waded into the water. It felt cold as it circled my ankles, then my knees. I held my breath as the icy water circled around my pelvis until I finally reached out and grabbed the fishing line that floated on the rippling water.

Success! After a couple of tugs I had freed the fishing line and dragged it out behind me as I made my way back to the shore.

"Ha! With your luck you'll probably catch two fish dragging your line through the water like that!" Wade yelled at me across the river.

I made my way back to the beach and pulled the tangled line up to the shore. Nope, Wade was wrong. I didn't catch two fish: I caught THREE!!

Wade frowned at me as the fish lay on the beach wiggling and twisting to get back to the water.

"Hmm," he mumbled and broke his line and started walking through the water. I can proudly say that I caught the biggest haul that day because for all his dragging, and river walking, Wade only caught two fish.

After the fishing lesson, we ate a modest picnic and lay on the blanket staring up at the clouds that drifted over our heads. Lost in thoughts of dreams and love we snuggled together and let the summer sun warm us.

"Let's go skinny dipping," Wade rolled over and smiled at me.

"No," I said, alarmed at the thought.

"Come on, it's hot out. There's no one around. No one will know."

Wade has always been able to twist me around his finger and

make me do whatever he wanted. I was a willing puppy to his stupidity. I watched my boyfriend strip down to his underwear and climb into a gentle flowing bay he had found. With a shrug I also stripped down to my panties and followed in behind Wade. He laughed as he saw me with my mask of uncertainty and shyness.

"Come here, angel," he whispered in my ear as he held me tight to his chest. I relaxed in his strong arms and let his warm kisses slide down my throat and across my shoulders. We played like lovers, like children, like best friends. We kissed, we laughed, we told silly stories about each other, we splashed and played tag until we grew tired and made our way back to our blanket.

We let the warm sun dry our skin until we could finally put our clothes back on. We kissed and held hands as we packed up our fishing camp; it was a perfect day.

The next day we decided to recapture that perfect moment with another trip to the river. We hurried down to the beach with our fishing gear in our arms. Coming up the beach were four of Wade's cousins; they also had spent the day fishing.

"Did you miss something?" Wade's female cousin held up my bra.

"It's not mine," I lied and blushed. In our haste to pack up the camp yesterday, I decided to not put my bra back on. Instead, I rolled it up in my towel. I guess it must have fallen out.

To this day, I suspect Wade's uncle is harboring my best bra in his house. Perhaps it is still laying in his dresser waiting for me to claim it. In my dreams I can hear my bra calling me, "Gina! Gina! Where are you? It's dark in here, and I'm frightened! When are you coming to get me?"

Like I said, the day trips just didn't turn out well and I had hoped this overnight trip would produce better results. Yeah, this trip was different, it actually included real packing of the house. We didn't have a tent, but my six-foot, one-inch boyfriend said we could sleep in the back of the car.

"There's lots of room," Wade exclaimed.

Food, pillows, blankets, food, pots and pans, and my boyfriend (the Human Compass), and we were off!

Travelling on the highway with my love of my life was a perfect moment. The sun shone through the windows, the wind rustled our hair, and the whole world seemed to exist just for us. Never in my life could I ever love anyone more than my Wade, although the conversation was a little odd for a boy who was to receive the "I am perfect" award from his girlfriend.

"Hey, were you ever scared of outhouses when you were a kid?" questioned Wade.

"Yeah, I suppose so. I used to think I was going to fall in," I admitted.

"I used to think rattlesnakes would slither up to the seat and bite me," said Wade.

"I used to think it was bees, or a hand from some monster who lived down there in the sewage and he would want me to live with him because he was lonely," I said.

"Huh!" Wade frowned at me. "You really have an overactive imagination, don't you, honey?"

"Baby, you don't know half of it," I laughed, because really he didn't. "Ever notice when you went to the outhouse that you can hear every footstep and noise, people breathing and talking, and yet when you go outside there is never anyone there?"

"Yeah. I heard noises once. I couldn't figure out where they were coming from. Scratching and running on the roof. I quickly did my business and walked outside. No one was there. I started to walk away and heard the scratching on the outhouse roof, I turned and saw a squirrel running up the tree beside the outhouse."

"Spooked over a squirrel. It could happen to anyone; the important thing is you're safe now," I patted Wade's hand and smiled. "I always liked the outhouses with the green PVC roof. When you come out the whole world is pink."

"I remember those. Did I ever tell you about my outhouse story?"

"What outhouse story?" I frowned at the question.

"Well, I see I never told you. Well, when I was younger I went camping with some buddies of mine. Every night we would go one by one to the outhouse before we went to bed. My one buddy would always carry the flashlight so we could see where we were going. One night he carried the flashlight to the outhouse and left it on the ledge by the seat. Well, it accidentally fell into the crapper. He came running out begging us to get it back for him."

"What did you do?" I asked.

"We told him to forget it. It's gone! No way in hell that's coming back, you know."

"So then what happened?"

"Nothing. It stayed in the crapper. We were all really impressed with its batteries. It lit up our asses for two days straight."

"Wade, what was the point of this story?" I answered, annoyed.

"Point? Why does anything have to have a point? Why can't you just tell a story that's pointless?"

"All stories have to have a point. People become disillusioned if you have no point," I answered.

"Well, I guess the point of my story is that it's better to buy Duracell batteries."

"Why is that?"

"Because it could have lit up our asses for weeks instead of two days."

Did I mention that my boyfriend was perfect? Well, in light of the outhouse story I had to revise my opinion, he was almost perfect. In fact over the years I would learn that Wade has a strange aversion to clothes hampers. He can stand right in front of one and still dump his clothes on the floor. He also uses every pan and dish in the house when he's cooking and runs out the door every time, leaving me with the mess. However, despite all the little annoying habits he has, I love him to pieces.

Moonshine Lake is approximately twenty-four kilometers northeast of Dawson Creek, BC. As I drove enjoying the scenery and my boyfriend had now gone to another topic, which thankfully did not include outhouses, I began to realize that we were approaching our required distance and still my boyfriend (the Human Compass) hadn't said anything. In fact, by the puzzled look on his face, I'd say he looked like a man who is lost.

"Are we lost?" I finally broke down and asked.

"No. I know exactly were we are," Wade reassured me.

I kept driving east. It seemed hours had clicked by. Surely, twenty-four kilometers couldn't take this long?

"Wade, are you sure?" I asked again.

"Positive. I told you I grew up here. I've been here a hundred times!" Wade exclaimed.

I kept driving. I was getting worried; we would reach the Alberta border soon.

"Wade, are we lost?" I asked again, exasperated.

"No. Not really," Wade answered quietly.

"What does 'No, not really' mean?"

"It means we're only slightly lost," Wade replied.

At this point I had enough! I pulled over to the side of the road and looked at my boyfriend. I wanted a straight answer from the Human Compass.

"Wade, this is really important. Are we lost?" I questioned firmly.

Wade looked out the window as if looking for a familiar landmark. After a moment of quiet thought, he turned to me and said, "Yes, we're lost."

"Now what!" I yelled.

"Turn around and go back. I saw a campsite someplace back up the highway," Wade ordered.

The decision was made by the navigator to retreat. Thinking that I didn't want to spend the night sleeping on the side of the highway, I turned the car around and drove back down the highway to find the elusive campground.

It was after supper when we finally arrived in the campsite. We found the perfect spot right up against the tree line. It was quiet and clean. I pulled in the car and Wade and I set up a camp for the night. Wade chopped the wood as I unrolled the blankets and set up something that could form a bed for the both of us. Before long there was a crackling fire and we were both huddled up on the bench, keeping warm as we shared a bag of Cheesies (Wade's favorite snack). Lost, as if in a dream, I put my head on Wade's shoulder and drifted away.

"Look, a bear!" Wade pointed to a small black animal on the roadway.

In all the years I had been camping in the mountains I had only seen a wild bear three or four times. The bears were always in a hurry to leave all the attention they were getting so I never got a close-up look at one. I squinted to get a better look.

"That's a dog," I replied. (Honest, from this distance it really did look like a dog.)

"I've seen hundreds of bears, Gina. I know a bear when I see one," Wade growled at me.

I looked up at my boyfriend and frowned. I didn't know if I should trust him. I mean, this is the same guy who promised me a lake at his old stomping grounds and look at how that turned out.

I decided to get a closer look.

Bears generate a lot of attention. I know when I used to go to the zoo there was always a lot of people at the bear den. Bears are impressive. A huge four-legged animal that can stand on its hind end. Long ferocious fangs and powerful claws that can tear metal in a car and rip apart a human in a matter of seconds. A loud, deafening roar that can ripple through your body and leave you weak. Now a wild bear can gain even more attention as they leave you breathless with excitement as you wait for them to rip apart the neighbor's trailer or drag off the carcass of a deer. Mostly, nothing happens. Bears, although dangerous and ferocious, are more scared of you and normally run for the bushes.

In my case Wade noticed the bear and so did a family traveling on the highway. Apparently, a family travelling in a car spotted the yearling black bear crossing the highway and running off into the ditch. The anonymous family then followed the little guy to get a closer look; this frightened the baby bear into running into the campsite. That poor baby, I'll never forget the look of fear on his face. All he wanted to do was escape. Unfortunately he decided to escape right through our camp.

"Get in the car!" Wade ordered, as the baby bear came running towards us.

I did as I was told. I threw my Cheesies bag in the air and bolted for the car. I heard stories of mutilations, face graphs, screaming (oh, the screaming), all from the expense of a frightened bear. If you go hiking and encounter a bear in its territory, it may frighten you by running up to you, it may let out an earth-shattering roar and pound the ground with its front paws and leave, or it may kill you. A frightened bear that is being chased will just kill you, there is no roar and warning. You are just dead. That's it! Game over!

I didn't want to be a horrible mutilation story. I liked my face the way it was, so I dove into the car. It was then I realized I left the axe outside and I had no way to protect myself. (Of course, it never dawned on me that you can't swing an axe INSIDE of a car, but I was frightened.) I turned scared to my darling, my love of my life, my beloved, my rock … to find the rock was outside laughing his butt off. He thought the scared look on my face and throwing the Cheesies in the air was hysterical. (I will always wonder why does it seem amusing to men to see woman who are panic-stricken and frantic?) Then calmly Wade got off the bench and opened the car door and got inside the car.

"I just remembered I could be eaten too," Wade said, and locked the door behind him.

The bear ran beside our car and into the bushes in front of us. All the fear and danger was over in a matter of a few seconds. I wanted to get a closer look at the little fur baby, but all I could see was Wade's arms flying around in the car as he demonstrated over and over again how I threw those Cheesies in the air, followed by, "Honey, you should've seen the look on your face," Wade laughed. (Yep, it was going to be a long night at my expense)

Now I have slept many times in the back seat of a car. Once my parents were traveling in the mountains and it was getting late and all the campsites were full so we slept in the car, Mom and Dad in the front seat, us kids wildly thrown about in the back seat. It was a long night and a really uncomfortable and cramped sleep. Now I had never slept with a six-foot, one-inch man before. This was a lot different that being twelve years old and sharing a car seat with my skinny fourteen-year-old sister.

As I unrolled the blankets I had it all mapped out in my mind. If Wade sleeps on his side, puts one arm under my pillow, one leg on my hip, and the other arm over my waist, THIS JUST MIGHT WORK! (I am a genius, just like my father.)

Wade curled up on his side and held me tight to his chest. We fell asleep as soon as our heads hit the pillows. All night long I dreamt of leather saddles that needed polishing, leather boots that came in my size, leather purses on sale, leather jackets ... leather ... leather. I smelled leather. I opened one eye. All I could see was red. There was a good reason to see red. That was because my face was pressed tightly against the back of my leather seat. I wedged myself away from Wade and balanced myself on the edge of the seat on one hip. I turned and looked down at Wade. Apparently the term "lots of room" applies only to him, as I watched my boyfriend spread himself out and snore so loud the windows vibrated. I managed to nudge Wade over so I had a pocket of room. Sleep finally came, but it was not a restful one as the sunlight filled up our car at five o'clock in the morning. Still tired, we packed up our camp and drove back to our apartment. There was no time to unpack, no conversation, no laughter as we dragged our sore and cramped bodies up the flight of stairs to our apartment door.

There was only the sound of snoring as Wade and I fell into bed. It had been another misadventure, but a good misadventure.

CHAPTER TEN

1990: MARRIED LIFE WITH THE SUNSHINE BIBLE CAMP

When I was little I used to dream of my wedding. I think all little girls do. We are conditioned from our mothers, who repeatedly tell us, "One day you will get married and have babies." There is no way out for you. Well, there was no way out for me as I dreamt of a love, an unconditional love, that would take me away from my lonely existence and make me a home in a penthouse suite overlooking a fabulous, exciting city.

I would grab the bed sheet off my bed and wrap it around my waist as I practiced walking with a dress and train in my bedroom. Then there was the honeymoon. Staring off into each other's eyes, as we walked down the beaches of Waikiki.

"Yes, the sunset over the palm trees is lovely," I would imagine myself saying.

"Not as lovely as you," my imaginary husband would reply. His husky voice and dark eyes told me of his lust and passion for me.

But this is real life. The man I married was a thin boy, who was barely getting paid as a chef in a popular restaurant. He has ambition, courage, an enormous amount of talent, and dedication, and it all went unnoticed by his employers. I had only a fragment of what I had asked for in a perfect partner. I got the loving husband who looks at me with passion. For me that was enough. It didn't matter to me that Wade was poor. To me he was perfect.

My mother always said, "You can't survive on love." Well, you can. Love can hold you together in all the dramatic moments of your life, it can hold you together in all the saddest moments of your life, it can glue together all the broken parts and rebuild a new start. All love needs is time, because in time all things can get better.

No, money didn't matter to me. All I wanted was to be loved. What good was money if the man you shared it with didn't love you? No, I figured it was better to be poor and loved than rich and unloved. So when my husband-to-be said he couldn't afford an expensive honeymoon, maybe just some camping, I promised to love that boy with every breath in my body. All that mattered to me was the people I cared deeply for.

"Sure, camping would be fine," I answered. I was a little sad that I was trading grass skirts for camp coffee, but I knew Wade was offering his heart.

Now prior to my wedding my mother let slip to relatives that we were camping for our honeymoon. So my wedding gifts consisted of one huge cooler, two medium coolers, and a small cooler. One water jug; one juice jug; two lanterns to see in the dark; a picnic basket with plastic plates, cups, and utensils; a bottle of peach vodka; camp mats; camp pillows; backpacks; and an inflatable sink to wash my camp dishes. In fact, there was very little to furnish my small apartment with. However, whoever was camping beside us would be greatly impressed with all the matching camp supplies.

After the wedding Wade and I drove south up the highway to Calgary. We made an overnight stop in Calgary and, in the morning, the zoo. We took tons of pictures of our perfect day and soon we were on our way to Banff. I was happy this time to be in our two-man tent. I curled up beside my new husband. I was so content and so deeply in love as we fell asleep in each other's arm. I didn't even mind the drizzle of rain that dripped on the roof of our tent.

It was probably around two o'clock in the morning when the drizzle of rain became an outright downpour. I curled up with Wade on the only dry spot left. In the more decent hours of the morning it became more apparent that we had a major problem. The tent, our pillows, sleeping bags, and pajamas were all soaked from the early morning rain.

"What are we going to do now?" Wade grumbled as he held up our soggy tent.

"Well, we can hang it on a tree limb and wait for it to dry," I suggested.

"I don't want to hang out here all day waiting for the damn tent to dry."

"I guess we'll just have to roll it up wet."

Wade and I began the process of packing up the camp when a wave of dizziness came over me.

"You ok?" my husband frowned at me.

"I don't know. I must be getting sick."

"Did you eat breakfast?"

"Yeah. I'm probably just getting a cold from last night's rain," I admitted.

"Maybe tonight we'll stay in a hotel."

"But honey, we don't have much money and hotels are expensive."

"Look, I'm worried about you, and our gear is wet anyways," said Wade.

I packed up the rest of our camp with the matter now being settled. We decided to travel back up the highway and get as close to Jasper as possible. The day was perfect. The sun shone and the green grass waved by the side of the road. The goats made their way down from the mountain and greeted the tourists who stopped to take their picture; we hiked through trails and stopped for lunch at the Columbian Icefields. I was in a world of young love. Time seemed to stop every time Wade laughed and smiled. I wanted to capture a photograph in my mind whenever Wade's eyes sparkled. I wanted to take all the feeling I had in my soul and cocoon Wade and me for all eternity. Every moment was so perfect.

By the evening, we found a fairly reasonable hotel room. That is to say, we still had money for breakfast in the morning. Normally we would never consider a hotel but it was an emergency. I was still not feeling well and the camp gear was still soaked. We spread our tent over a chair, our blankets over a table, and the pillows in the window case in an effort to get them dry. It worked!! By morning the camp was ready to be set up again.

That afternoon we were back on the road again, this time making our way slowly towards Grande Prairie. We made it as far as Grand Cache and stopped for the night. It was during the setup that Wade, my poor darling, realized he forgot his jacket at the hotel.

"Was your wallet in your coat?" I asked him while pitching the tent.

"No, something much worse."

"What's worse than losing your wallet?"

"My good set of darts were in the upper left pocket. I loved those darts," Wade admitted.

"I'll buy you another set when I get home," I scowled at Wade.

"It'll never be the same," Wade sighed and sat down at the picnic table. He looked like a boy who just lost his dog.

"It'll be fine," I patted his shoulder.

"No, it never will be fine again," Wade stared off into space. I thought perhaps it would be best to leave him with his thoughts; in time he'll get over it. (I was wrong, sixteen years later Wade can recall losing those darts better than the honeymoon.)

I stood back and admired my homemaking skills in a campsite. A decorative checkered cloth on the table, a nice tablecloth touch, and a glass full of wildflowers. Two blue plastic dishes for place settings, and our large coolers neatly displayed under the picnic table. A spot close to the lake (don't ask me which one, because I don't know. Apparently my husband had the same gypsy genes as my father.), close to the bathrooms, and close to the beach. It was a shady spot with large trees and large bullfrogs. Yes, the whole place was perfect. If only I felt better.

"Still got the flu?" Wade patted my back.

"Yes," I swooned. "It was that stupid rain storm."

"Do you want to go hiking?"

"No. Not right now. I don't like the heat," I confessed.

"Fine!" Wade yelled and threw his hat on the ground in anger. "What a great honeymoon!"

I tried to feel bad. I really did, but the flu had my mind clouded and all I could think and feel was sick. I crawled into the tent and lay down gently on the sleeping bags.

By evening time, I could sit up again. I could even eat a few bites of food. I even cuddled my grumpy new husband. As the hours drifted away our thoughts turned to something more intimate. Soft gestures and touches indicated passion was on the horizon. That was until our new neighbors showed up in the campsite next to us.

It was a bus.

It was a bus full of kids.

It was a bus full of kids from camp.

It was a bus full of kids from the Sunshine Bible Camp.

As the doors flew open, kids from the ages of thirteen to sixteen ran off the bus and assembled tents. THEY WERE EVERYWHERE!!!! They were only five feet away and could hear "EVERYTHING" that Wade and I said (and did).

"This could be a problem," Wade sat down beside the fire with me.

"A major problem," I replied.

"I thought we could … you know," Wade nudged me shyly.

"I know. I thought we could also … you know," I said. I was very disappointed. What kind of a honeymoon was this turning into when you couldn't … you know? But I really didn't want to share my love life with thirty kids. In the evening, Wade and I cuddled close around a crackling fire, cups of cocoa to keep us warm against the damp evening air.

"Maybe we can just … you know, quietly. No one will hear us," Wade suggested.

"Yeah. It could work," I responded, and kissed my husband.

Slowly the kisses deepened and our hearts began to pound, as blood rushed through our bodies. We stopped and smiled at each other; love was shining in our eyes. Wade kissed me again and I wound my hands through his hair and pulled him closer to me. I could feel all the muscles in Wade's body straining to get closer. That's about where the kids from camp started singing.

"Seek ye first the kingdom of God and his righteousness. And all these things will be added unto you. Allelu, allelu, alleluia."

"Just pretend you don't hear it," Wade kissed me harder and clamped his hands over my ears.

I tried. I really tried, but it was no use. The kids just sang louder with each kiss we gave each other. Now I don't know how many of you out there have encountered the talented voices of the Sunshine Bible Camp, but I can tell you from personal experience that nothing kills the passion faster than thirty kids in unison singing, "Alice the camel has ten humps. Alice the camel has ten humps. Alice the camel has ten humps, so GO Alice GO! Boom! Boom! Boom!"

"Maybe we'll stay at a hotel tomorrow," said Wade as he crawled into bed with me that night.

"Good idea," I replied.

We stuffed tissue in our ears that night and put pillows over our heads to drown out the singing choir. Wade rolled over and gave me a quick kiss good night and faced the wall of the tent. I shut my eyes, but even with stuffed ears and a pillow over my head, I could still hear the kids singing. Finally they all went to sleep and I could too.

Sunshine filled our little tent and Wade and I opened our eyes to greet the new day. Cuddled up, we made the decision to get the heck out of there before the Sunshine Bible Camp woke up.

We stuck our heads out the door and surveyed the layout. It was too late!!! WE WERE SURROUNDED!!! The kids walked through our camp! They walked all over the table! They walked on the edges of our tent! Thirty kids all heading back and forth from the washroom.

"Let's get out of here!" Wade shouted back to me.

I didn't reply, I was already packing up the camp. In fact if there was a Guinness Book of Records for fastest camp pack-up I would've won it that day. Before you know it, we were back on the road again.

Wade growled and snarled at me for miles. If it wasn't bad enough he lost his good set of darts, had missed his breakfast, and had no ... you know, his plans for a romantic honeymoon were being squashed with me being sick.

"Maybe a camping honeymoon wasn't such a great idea after all," Wade growled.

I didn't reply. I didn't dare. I wanted to keep my head on my shoulders. I put my head on the car window and watched the scenery go by. I was starting not to feel well again.

It was around noon when we checked into the Grande Prairie Hotel. It was lovely. For forty-five dollars a night for a double occupancy room, it was a real gem of a find. It had gourmet dining, a pool, a lovely clean room, with a double bed. I looked towards the window, it had air conditioning — alleluia! I turned it on and flopped on the bed.

"Not feeling well again?" Wade asked as he set our luggage down on the floor.

"I just can't seem to shake this flu," I admitted. The room started to spin again.

"When we get home, you should go see the doctor."

I looked up into the worried eyes of my husband. I gave him a little reassuring smile.

"I'll be fine. Whatever it is, it will just have to work itself out," I said.

"No. I think there's something wrong. Maybe the doctor can give you something to settle your stomach," Wade rubbed my back lovingly.

I admit I really didn't care if there was a rectal probe involved, I just wanted the room to stop spinning and be able to eat a meal and keep it down.

The next day Wade and I were home again. Our first stop was to see the doctor; we waited nervously as the doctor gave us our test results.

"You're not sick," my doctor told me. "Congratulations, you kids are pregnant."

"So the twelve pregnancy tests we did in the Grande Prairie Hotel were not defective after all," I said to Wade.

Even after all the testing, Wade and I were still shocked. We never planned a family so soon. By the time we made it to the car, we were smiling. Then it turned into giggling. When we drove up the driveway to our apartment, we were laughing. We couldn't believe it; we were going to be parents to our child. We created a life. A baby. A baby. A perfect little baby.

My mother often said that families are like a wheel. The parents are the hub of the wheel, the children the spokes, and the grandchildren are the rubber that goes on forever.

On March 8, 1991, at 7:30 p.m., Zackeriah came into the world. All pink and perfect with ten fingers and ten toes, a son.

On December 11, 1993, at 8:30 p.m., Ryan found his way into his family. A large baby, a king, screaming and kicking his way into existence with a mother to adore him and a father to love him.

Our family was complete.

By being born, Zack and Ryan had given Wade and me our own wheel. Everything we do or say now affects the lives of these two little people.

"Camping is going to be a lot more fun," Wade smiled at his boys, now ages two and four playing in the living room.

"We're going to need a bigger tent," I suggested.

"I'll go shopping for one," said Wade. He leaned back in his chair with a dreamy look in his eyes.

I stood back and admired my family. My husband sat in his chair, all dreamy with visions of camping and fishing in his mind, while my children fed grapes to each other off the coffee table. I agreed with Wade. Camping was going to be a lot more fun. Not that it wasn't fun with just Wade, but now I could live through my children's eyes.

Everything I have seen and done a hundred times will all be new to them. I had so much to show them, and I could hardly wait.

CHAPTER ELEVEN

1998: LAKE SWIMMING AND DAIRY ANIMALS

When you camp with kids, you no longer have a holiday just for yourself. It now becomes all for the kids. Healthy menu plans you may have had for yourself are now replaced with Pokemon noodles, canned stew, pop, and a variety of junk food. Out goes the idea of the resort lifestyle plans you may have had, instead you find yourself travelling down nowhere highways to see Flintstoneland and the world's largest pierogi.

The first time Zack, my oldest son, went on a camp trip, he was six months old. I was so worried that my tiny baby would freeze in the night that I wrapped him in several blankets and built him a bed of pillows, and put him just above my head so I could reach him in the night and kept checking to see if he was still warm. In the night my baby would cry and I would search the blankets trying to figure out what was wrong. Was he warm? Was he hungry? Was he wet? Nope, this time Zack had soiled his diaper, and he needed a change.

"Wade, wake up," I nudged my sleeping husband.

"What is it?" Wade opened his groggy eyes and tried to focus on me in the dark tent.

"Zack needs his diapers changed."

"So, change them!" Wade growled and turned over and went to sleep.

I looked at Wade's back in the dark, he had fallen back to sleep. I was on my own. I shook my head. Why is it men have the best five minutes of their lives, and it is us women who end up carrying the baby with sore backs, bloated bladders, swollen feet, and not to mention the painful stage of childbirth, but also the years of raising the child and changing diapers?

"Oh, forget it," I told myself and grabbed Zack and started to peel him from the blankets like a banana. After several minutes of unwrapping I finally found my pink, warm little baby and removed his diaper. Zack gurgled and cooed in my arms as I sought a fresh diaper I had piled up beside my pillow. I gently lay my fragile baby back down and slipped the fresh cloth under his adorable little bottom. I slipped my hand under his bottom, to make sure the diaper was under him properly, when something warm and squishy pressed up against my hand.

"Geez! Geez!" I cried out in alarm.

"What the hell is it?" Wade woke up in a panic. He too was alarmed from my yelling.

"Zack pooped all over my hand!" I cried.

"Oh, is that all," Wade stated and rolled back over and fell back to sleep again.

Like I said, men are only there for five minutes of fun. Zack's dirty diaper reminded me to always bring a lantern, and to never diaper a baby in the dark.

When you camp as a family for the first time, it becomes one of the most important memories of your life. You will notice that your child has anxieties. Your child realizes that there is life beyond home, and that a tent can be a home as long as loving parents are there. It is a chance for your child to observe, explore, encounter, and understand within a safety ring.

My father was the king of the campsite, but my husband is the king of the overnight camping adventure. We have pitched our four-man tent at Bellis Lake, Hasse Lake, Star Lake, Mons Lake, Good Fish Lake, Sir Winston Churchill Park, and others to many too mention. Wade is a good man, a loving man, but he's a man on limited time to do anything with his family. "Sorry, honey, I gotta go" is Wade's standard line as every day he runs off to work. "Sorry, honey, I can't mow the lawn, gotta go." "Sorry, honey, I can't help you paint the house, or take out the trash, or fix the car, gotta go." Well, this sort of thing now has interrupted our camping trips. We're off Sunday and back Monday, because Wade has to be back to work on Tuesday. All he can give us is one night. Over the years, we expect this from Wade. However, we still try to change things.

"Can't you take some time off?" I begged.

"Sure I can, but they are short-handed at work. If I leave now they will really struggle," said Wade as he put on his chef uniform.

"You know it's like this everywhere you have ever worked. They're short-handed. They can't work without me. Can't we just take off and go somewhere?"

"Sure, maybe in a couple of months we can take four days off."

"Four days!!!!" I exclaimed. "Wade, please, can't we take off a couple of weeks?"

"Nope. Sorry, honey. I told you we had a couple of guys quit on us and I have to help out. You know how it is."

"Sure," I sulked. Of course I knew how it was. I was married to the man for eight years now and I got to know the restaurant industry pretty good. I know how inventory runs, how menus are planned, how food standards are essential, how management works, and how customer service is performed because my Wade taught me. I just didn't think it was fair that a man with all his diplomas and certificates in food service and management always had to be the guy that companies never promoted and yet was such a devoted company man. Wade devoted his life to running to work, why couldn't he run to me a little? "You know, Wade, one day you will come home from work and the boys will be grown up and gone. You should spend more time with them before it's too late."

"Look," Wade sighed and sat down on the bed beside me. "If it means that much to you, I'll see what I can do about taking a few days off next week, ok?"

"Ok," I brightened up. "I'll start packing."

"Sure, whatever makes my little girl happy," Wade gave me a kiss and looked at his watch. "Oh, sorry, honey, I gotta go. I'm going to be late."

I swear I am going to have those words etched on that man's tomb. Over the years my boys would refer their father as the white rabbit in *Alice in Wonderland*. "I'm late. I'm late. For a very important date. No time to say hello, goodbye. I'm late. I'm late. I'm late." If only Wade ran to me like he does to his job every day. Heck, if only he worked as hard at home, like he does at work, I'd be happy.

"Well, no use daydreaming," I told the empty room. "I have packing to do."

Overnight trips have been a strain on me. Packing up the entire house and trying to make it all fit in the trunk of a two-door 1984 Mustang is no easy task. In fact, it seems like such an enormous amount of energy wasted for one little overnight trip, but that is all I ever got and I am not the type of person to let opportunity to travel anyplace slip by.

It was no easy feat, but I managed to pack up an entire camp, and two kids and my husband, in that cramped little car.

"Our family is growing," said Wade.

"Yes, it is," I sighed. I was tired from all the packing, while Wade entertained the boys by watching TV in the house.

"We should look into a bigger vehicle," Wade suggested.

"I agree."

Our family had become bigger, by at least two dogs.

In the summer of 1998, we got Kenny, a purebred basset hound. Red and white in color with stubby little legs and long ears that he sometimes tripped over, and a disgusting drool problem, Kenny was the light of my life. He had been pushed around to a few homes before he came to live with us. I promised Kenny we would be his last home and that he would live a good life with us and be treated with respect and dignity and he was, until his death in 2001 from cancer.

Kenny was easy to train. In no time at all I had him sit, lay down, roll over, jump up (sort of, on those little legs), stay, come, and bark. Like I said, Kenny was easy to train, but to my boys Kenny's most impressive feature was his sometimes eye-watering farts that had you open all the windows and abandon ship. I think Kenny was very impressed with it too, because every time that dog farted, I swear he was smiling.

A year after Kenny came to live with us, a neighbor announced he was moving and could not take his dog with him. He asked we take Jasmine off his hands. I was happy too, because I love animals and I would do anything to give them a loving home if they needed one. In fact, Wade refuses to take me to the SPCA, because he said I'd bring all the animals home and he'd go broke trying to feed them all. Still my little Jasmine was a pleasure to have as an additional family member. Like Kenny, she was a purebred basset hound, only Jasmine had longer legs and shorter ears, and was tricolored. Smart as a whip that puppy was. She could beg, bark, sit, come, stay, roll over, jump down, even go through a hoop. Jasmine was my best friend, until her death in February 2007 from a severe stroke that paralyzed her. I really miss her.

With all these animals and people, the four-man tent was overcrowded. At one point I woke up in the morning in a pillow of fur. I sat up to realize the dog was sitting on my face. The car was becoming a problem too. Kenny sat on the floor of the car, under my feet, while Jasmine sat, ever a lady, in the back seat between the boys.

We simply needed a bigger vehicle.

In 1999, we bought a van. It was a 1984 Ford Aerostar. It was second-hand (naturally) and had every part in the engine replaced, but it ran well. Two-toned blue, with grey seats that could easily fit six people. It was enough room for two boys and their dogs.

The best part was realizing that when one bench seat was removed, the floor space was enough room to act as a bed. So my mind formed a plan that involved Wade and I camping in the van and the boys outside the door in the tent. Finally, no rain on my head, no damp clothes, oh what luxury! Problem was the boys thought it was luxury too and refused to sleep in the tent.

"Now where to put everybody?" I muttered to myself.

Ryan was small and slept on a mat in the trunk area. Zack slept on the only remaining bench seat left in the van. Wade and I slept on the open floor space, and the dogs took the driver and passenger seats up front. There! Room for everyone.

Wade and I decided to take our new camping arrangements to Lac La Biche and Sir Winston Churchill Park.

It was the year 2000 when we packed up and made our way up north. I watched miles and miles of gorgeous scenery pass by my windows. My eyes wandered across yellow farming fields of thick canola and stunning pine trees that made up a natural acidic rain forest. There were orange wild tiger lilies that grew in the ditches with pink fireweed standing as a guard over them. It was a magnificent painting easily a natural rival to any landscape by Monet. The blue sky and soft clouds drifted dreamily across the sky, looking down at all the earth from so far above. Magnificent! Wonderful! Spectacular!

After four hours of travel and several rest stops for bathroom breaks and junk food buying, we finally made it to Lac La Biche. I can't say that Lac La Biche is a very beautiful little town. In fact it is rather plain and dull in my opinion. Like time had forgotten this place. It stands lonely and unloved. What the town lacks in beauty it makes up in kindness. The people of Lac La Biche are funny, warm-hearted, and good people who serve a great cup of coffee in their local café. This very old town is surrounded by a gorgeous lake with an island that is reserved for camping. It is a remarkable place to vacation.

The campsite boasts 100 spots to pitch a tent, park a trailer, or set up your RV. It also had electrical outlets, full facility bathrooms, and a gorgeous lake to canoe, swim, or fish in.

However, the star attraction (or at least to me it was) was the pelicans that make their home here on this lake. I'll never forget the first time I saw them drifting aimlessly down the shoreline, so white and ancient in appearance. They seemed almost dinosaur in form, a pterodactyl of the past.

In a flock of twenty they came. First ten birds would fill the inner circle, while the other ten birds paddled their feet frantically in the outer circle. This frenzied stir of the water would excite any fish that lay along the shoreline, then the ten inner circle birds would eat their fill. Soon the birds would switch places and this would ensure everyone had food to eat in the flock: a perfect example of community spirit and a sure way to ensure the survival rate. I felt so very fortunate at having been a witness to this marvel of nature.

There is very little that one could complain about this park. The fees were only ten dollars a night and the people have a wonderful small-town community spirit. The only downfall that I could see was that you had to pay five dollars for an armload of wood. Now that might not seem like much, but I remember when you didn't pay for campfire wood at all. There used to be a time when all you paid for was the campsite fee; the rest was complementary.

"Gina, it's no big deal," Wade would sigh and dump the wood on the ground.

"It is a big deal, honey. I mean figure this out. This is dried wood and it burns very quickly. One armful for every meal of the day. So that's fifteen dollars a day. Then, times that by seven days of the week. It comes out to … $105, and then there's the camp fee, which is ten dollars a night times that by seven days a week so that's a total of $175 for the week."

"Gina, you are beginning to sound like your father."

"Oh, my God, I am. I have finally come full circle," I gasped.

"What do you mean?"

"Well, there is this moment when children become exactly like their parents. This must be my moment."

"Whatever, you nut," Wade laughed at me.

"Look, I'm just pointing out that it is a high price to pay for a product you burn and never see again."

"Honey, I need you to focus. I only have enough wood for a quick meal, there is not enough here to have a lingering campfire before we go to bed tonight."

"Oh, no," I moaned. It was true, we only had enough wood for a small meal fire. We had missed the log man when we were out looking at pelicans. Now what do we do? We can't borrow wood from a neighbor, since you have to pay for wood nowadays. It feels too awkward to buy wood off a stranger. So there is no choice, you have to drag it out of the bushes.

"There's no choice. We'll have to drag it out of the bushes," said Wade. (See I told you, there was no choice.)

Now parks don't like you to do that, because (and this is the most important point) they don't make more money off you. The second reason being that they are selective about the trees they cut down. The third is that wood left in the bush is home for wildlife, but we were desperate. We were starving, and the laws of the jungle say "Eat or be eaten," and there was no way any of us were going to give up our lives to be some predator's meal. (Squirrels are murderous when hungry, you know.)

Even my dogs knew this fact. Every day my dogs went on squirrel patrol. They hardly ate or slept. All day and all evening long they would stare up at the trees, a vacant expression in their tired eyes. I told my family we had to go home soon, before the dogs collapsed from exhaustion. As soon as we got home, I gave the dogs both a puppy cookie as medals of their active valiant duty to guard and protect us.

I watched Wade drag a log out of the bushes and chop it up with an axe. In a few minutes a radiating fire filled up the evening sky. The smell of wood and stew filled our nostrils. I sat down at the picnic table and sighed. Not everything can be perfectly planned.

Like the time I made moussaka. It came out a little runny.

"It's more like soupsaka," Ryan told me. "In fact, Mom, if you were in a moussaka contest, you probably won't win."

I looked at the runny tomato and cheese dish. It was harsh words, I know, but in retrospect Ryan was probably right. It was pretty awful. Nope, no matter how hard you try, you can't plan perfect.

With the fire in full blaze, a supper of wieners, canned noodles, coffee, and marshmallows was consumed. After supper Wade and I boiled up a pot of water and washed down the children and ourselves. That night Wade and I nestled our family into their beds and let our dreams drift out the van windows. There were a million stars in the sky that night. It was moment not meant for words, because there were no words to describe how truly beautiful it was.

Just above my head I could feel Ryan wiggling in his sleeping bag.

"Ryan, settle down and go to sleep," warned Wade.

For a brief moment Ryan was still, then the wiggling started again. Having wiggling bored children is all part of the package of having kids. Since this action is performed a hundred times a day, you get used to the wiggling and struggling, but this time it was annoying since it was rocking the van.

"Ryan, I said settle down!" Wade warned again

"I can't," my three-year-old replied.

"Why not? What's wrong?" I asked.

"Because there's a raccoon down my pants," Ryan laughed.

Everyone in the van burst into laughter. Ryan laughed the hardest, as if he told us the world's funniest joke. Ryan always was the comedian of the family. When he was four he memorized all the Halloween jokes left on the paper placemat at McDonald's. When people asked him his name, Ryan replied, "My name is Johnson." I had a lot of explaining to do with people, telling them his name is Ryan not Johnson. I consider myself very blessed that I have a family with a wonderful sense of humor, it is not often that people laugh at themselves. I have a great family that way.

I lay awake for a while looking up at the stars and listening to my family breathe in and out. Finally when I couldn't stay awake any longer, I closed my eyes and fell asleep too.

In the morning it was a fresh start to a new day. My husband quickly built a fire to start breakfast, and while I went through the boxes to find something to eat my children played in the trees like wilderness-born monkeys. There was a lightness that morning. No one talked of bills, money, television, shoes, jobs, or the house. All those stresses just seemed to drift away. My children played with exuberance and energy, their laughter and joy rang through the forest. They felt the lightness too. It was with that same sort of high spirit that we packed up our camp and turned out onto the highway once again.

The wind whistled through the windows and ruffled our hair as we leaned out the windows to admire the scenery around us.

"Look, Mom, a dairy horse!" Zack cried out from the back seat.

Wade and I laughed as we saw a black-and-white horse running across a grassy green pasture.

"There is no such thing as dairy horses, only cows," I explained.

This animal fact only opens up the doorway to more animal questions. Do brown cows give chocolate milk? How do geese know to fly south? If zebras are related to horses, who's related to a platypus? I have always tried to talk to my sons in a scientific, informative manner. I don't believe in the answer of God colored the sky with a large crayon and that is why the sky is blue. I explain about prisms and reflections of light and molecules of water. Children are sponges. They learn everything from their parents. How to talk, walk, and eat, and social behavior. I want my sons to be informative about the world around them, so I talk in a simplified adult language that they can understand. This type of question-and-answer forum can last several minutes with some families but with my sons it lasted from Lac La Biche to Lesser Slave Lake. I was so glad to get out of the van and set up camp. My head felt as if it had been sucked by a large vacuum. I haven't felt so probed since high school finals week. When children know you are a source of knowledge, they keep up a relentless line of questioning.

Lesser Slave Lake is the largest lake in Alberta. It covers an enormous area of 106 kilometers of water. On the east side of the lake there is a government campsite where I remembered staying once with my gypsy travelling parents. Wade and I decided to retrace that camp memory with an overnight stay at the same campsite. The problem with retracing anything by memory is that as you age, the memory fades. In short, we couldn't find it.

"How about this one?" Wade suggested as we drove into a private campground.

"Good enough," I replied.

We paid fifteen dollars for the one night and we were given

a site right on the sandy beach. RIGHT ON THE BEACH!!!! We couldn't believe our good luck. I'll never forget that one overnight trip. Sailboats drifted by the shoreline, their sails on parade with different colors like a mixed matched rainbow. My family walked in the shallow water and ran out to greet the small waves of water that crashed into our ankles. My children laughed as they body surfed the one-foot waves with full-length, inflatable plastic frogs. Wade and I held hands and enjoyed our children's pleasure. Sometimes in life, all that makes sense in this crazy world comes down to a single moment that you will carry in your heart forever. For me, it was the sight of my children laughing as the waves rocked them off their plastic frogs and into the water, and my husband diving into the water with all his clothes on. If God had said to me, "Gina, I will never give you more than this moment to bring you joy," I would have been happy with that.

Later we popped popcorn over a fire as a warm wind whistled through the willow trees. The orange sun kissed the lake and turned the beach into tangerine sand, as lovers walked hand in hand against the orange glow. My kids built several sand castles that night and found a large frog hopping through camp. Even my dogs had a wonderful evening. Kenny and Jasmine found a cool spot in the sand and slept as if they had been sharing coconut drinks on a tropical beach all day.

I have never been in a foreign country. I have never flown on a plane to some exotic location, where you sit in lounge chairs and drink fruit and alcohol with the little umbrellas on the side. I have always seen pictures of places like Mexico and Jamaica and wondered what it would be like.

To me, this lake with the orange sun and peach sand was like the pictures of Hawaii. It was a pity we only had the one night to enjoy it and discover it. I would have liked to stay longer to explore this paradise. Perhaps one day in the future, we will return.

I'd really like that.

CHAPTER TWELVE

1999: GRANDMA, ZOOS, AND HOODOOS

Vacations have gone up in price. When I was ten years old, the campsite was ten dollars a night, the park entrance to the Rocky Mountains was twenty dollars a week, and a hotel room was fifty dollars a night. Now, nineteen years later, the same campsite is $40 dollars a night, the park entrance is now $78 a week, and a hotel can cost as much as $120 a night (some are even more). Even firewood that used to be a free service can cost as much as twenty dollars an arm load.

For a young family, on a small budget, a summer holiday can sometimes be out of the question. For weeks my family sulked and grumbled around the house trying to figure out a way to improve our financial situation and take some well-deserved time off. There seemed to be no possible solution in sight, until one day my husband suggested I ask my mother if she might want to vacation with us.

This made sense to me. My husband adores my mom, my children adore my mom, and I've always been close to my mom, and she did say she wanted a holiday.

I asked my mom if she would like to join us on a pay-half-of-everything plan. She loved the idea.

Now planning takes skill, talent, many phone calls, and a destination.

My mom and I are planners. We plan our marriages, we plan our children's lives, we plan our own lives, and of course we plan our holidays.

"How about the mountains?" suggested Mom.

"Please. I think that trip has been done to death. Besides we don't have the money to go to that place. It's too expensive," I said.

"What about Kelowna? It's beautiful there."

"No, it's too far away, Mom. We only have a couple of days, we can't go too far away."

Decisions like this require more phone calls and deep thinking. We decided the trip should be fun for the children and really, really fun for the adults. So with careful planning we all decided on a trip to the Calgary Zoo and Drumheller Museum. Then came the division of money. Wade and I agreed to pay for gas, supper, and hotel for night. The next night it would mother's turn to pay for everything. Breakfast and lunches would be bought as groceries from the store and eaten in our hotel room and van. It was perfect! With expenses approved, rubber stamped, sworn on the chest of a passing boy scout, and voted in under oath of government assembly, we began to pack.

When I look back, I can't believe how easy it all was. We had so much fun that vacation. Supper was at a restaurant of our choice every night. Wade and I would choose one, and then Mother would have a turn. We ate in our room every morning, while gazing at the mountain view from our hotel window. We wandered in and out of all the little shops on the street and ate lunch in our van.

We drove ten minutes down the highway and went into the Calgary Zoo. We walked through the zoo gates with hundreds of other people. Bears, bats, kangaroos, dinosaur statues, and the best ice cream I ever had in my life were the highlights of that day.

It was evening time when we rolled into Drumheller and checked into a deserted motel just off the highway. We ate in a restaurant uptown and retired early on foam mattresses. I had a great sleep.

You see, I have this theory. I believe that all hotels and motels shop at the same uncomfortable mattress store. That is because checkout time is usually at eleven o'clock in the morning. I think that hotel and motel managers don't want you to be comfortable because you might accidentally sleep in and you might want to stay another night. They just don't want the hassle.

In the morning we all awoke to a commotion of people passing our door.

"Where is everybody going?" my mom asked as she opened the curtains to observe the throng of people all walking down the sidewalk to the restaurant in the building.

My mother is a real-life detective. When I lived in Calgary as a young woman, I had a young family that lived only two doors down from me. My mother sat in my rocking chair by the living room and watched the family leave their apartment and enter their car and leave for a few hours and then come back again. This constant coming and going every few hours all night long was a great puzzle and wonderful source of amusement to my mother.

"I think they're drug runners," she finally told me.

"I think you watch too much TV," I replied.

"Well, what else could they be doing? Back and forth all night long, who lives like that?"

"Well, maybe it's because they own the small restaurant down the street, Mom." Yep, like I said, my mom is a real detective. Sherlock Holmes is no match for my mom.

"Gina, have you seen so many vehicles?" my mom gasped.

Wade and I walked over to the motel window. Last night when we checked into the motel the place was virtually abandoned. This morning it was like a car sales lot. I had to agree with Mom, there was something odd going on. So many cars, and not a soul in sight.

We quickly dressed and packed up the car. With curiosity burning away in us, we walked down the sidewalk and made our way to the restaurant. It was packed. Every table was used up. It turned out the motel served an incredible buffet breakfast. So incredible it seemed that the entire town of Drumheller was there.

We waited a few minutes until a table was available. We ate well that morning. We knew we were violating the breakfast-in-our-rooms pact, but it was our last day on vacation and the smell of pancakes, waffles, bacon, sausages, hash browns, and eggs wafted through the air and into our stomachs.

With our bellies full, we wandered around the town for an hour or two and slowly made our way to the museum. The Tyrell Museum of Paleontology is the destination vessel of Drumheller. Millions of tourists go through the museum to discover the dinosaurs that have been unearthed in that area or that have been transported from foreign digs. Mother wandered slowly through the museum looking at all the different statues and displays. Wade and I, however, ran through the museum because we were busy chasing after our children, who thought the museum was the official tryouts for the Olympic track and field.

The day was lovely, and soon it was time to head home.

Outside of Calgary we were hit by a hard rain. It blinded us. It paralyzed us. For a few feet we followed the bumper of the vehicle in front of us.

"I have to pull over and stop," said Wade. "I'm afraid I might hit someone."

We pulled over to the side of the road. In seconds we were blinded with a sheet of white rain. It pounded so hard that at times it seemed as if it might crash right through the windshield. We all huddled up close together and prayed that the rain would stop soon.

Then as suddenly as it came, the rain left. We looked around us with surprise. In the rain, we thought we were the only ones on the side of the road terrorized by the violent rain. In actual fact there were forty-three parked cars on the side of the road. Inch by inch, the traffic started to move again.

Within four hours we were back in Edmonton again. The trip was over.

To this day, my mom still talks about that trip and how much fun she had.

To me, it was a personal time I spent with my mom. Sure, I have thousands of them. Mom's homemade bread, the cute giggle she has when she thinks something is funny, her jokes, her corny sense of humor, and her unquenchable thirst for British TV. This was different.

This memory is just mine. I don't have to share it with my brother or sister. It's my own treasure to keep.

In the years that followed, my family and my mother have vacationed in Prince Rupert, BC, for a whale adventure, and to Vancouver Island to tour the gorgeous gardens and museums, but that one trip to Drumheller and the zoo was the most memorable for us all.

CHAPTER THIRTEEN

2005: RVS AND ISLAND YOGOURT

In 2005, Wade and I sold our home and used a partial sum to purchase a 1983 Empress, a Chevy RV.

The first time I saw it, I knew it had potential. There was a pattern of brown checkers and daisy prints all over the place, but I knew it could be lovely. It just needed a little love, like a Charlie Brown Christmas tree.

It had an AM, CB, and FM radio. There was a small bathroom with a single sink, toilet, and shower. It had a table and bench that shifted into a bed, a fridge with a freezer, a stove, an oven, and a microwave. It had a single sink in the kitchen and lots of storage, a small couch that lifted into a full bed, and a bunk that folded out above the cab.

The RV is not very big, only twenty-one feet in length, but it suited us perfect.

We drove it home, and I began to decorate.

That's the wonderful part of being an artist: I have a good sense of color and imagination. I tore down the mixed matched patterns of material and replaced it with blue–and-white material with Japanese gardens and temples on it. I put up new white blinds with a blue valance, a TV with a new VCR and DVD player, new blue shower curtains with colorful fish dancing on it. I even put up blue wallpaper and white tiles around the sink.

What seemed like a dull little brown hovel now feels like a tranquil aquarium whenever you step in the door. I feel relaxed and peaceful in my new little home away from home.

It seemed like luxury. I was in heaven. I thought I had it all. Scenery rolling past my kitchen window, a well-designed living space, and good tires for solid travel. What more could I ask for?

"We need a utility trailer," informed Wade.

"What for?" I replied.

"Well, look at all the stuff we have acquired, honey."

Indeed it seemed like we had gathered a lot of stuff. A red Ram-X 15 Coleman canoe with paddles and life jackets. Two inflatable rubber rafts (in case the boys get tired of canoeing), four folding camp chairs, an outdoor stove, and mini BBQ. Two inflatable rubber lounge chairs with Homer Simpson decorated on the front. Torches with insect repellent, to light up the night and keep off the bugs. For my husband the fisherman, I have important fishing gear like hip waders, an angler's inflatable raft (I call it Wade's donut thingy), a collection of over ten fishing poles (Wade's pride and joy), and three tackle boxes.

Wade and I searched around and finally ended up with an older wooden utility trailer that we fixed up. It was the ultimate family recreation unit.

Too bad the RV broke down a month later.

Not being mechanically inclined, we ran from dealerships to garages to fix it.

At first it was that the tank didn't switch from one tank to another. It happened a few times that we were stranded on the side of the road and had to get towed to a gas station. Two garage visits later and the problem seemed to be solved. Then the battery drained all the time.

We would be driving and stop for propane (because the RV runs on propane) and the engine would be dead. We had to get quite a few boosts from some very nice people just to get home.

Enough was enough. I begged Wade to take action. We took it back to the garage.

"Well, it's not the battery," the mechanic told us.

"Then what is draining all the power?" asked Wade.

"You probably need a connector."

For three years Wade and I went to dealerships, RV wreckers, and countless garages hoping someone had a connector we could use and regain our holiday summer fun wagon. We wanted to go back to camping.

I have developed over the years what I call the evolution of camping. When you are young the only thing you can afford is a tent. The tent then is thrown over for something larger like a tent trailer or a camper because the family is growing. When the children have become teenagers, the tent trailer is sold and replaced by an RV. Then when the children have left home, you vacation by reservation in hotels.

Well, my children were teenagers and I was not ready for the last stage of vacation by reservation only. I wanted my RV back.

"Please, do something," I begged Wade. I wanted to travel again.

"I'm trying. I'm trying, honey, but I don't have the money to keep fixing it," Wade tried to sympathetically explain to me.

"Please, do anything."

Wade looked at my pitiful face and his heart broke. On a suggestion from my brother Wade went out and bought a new battery. The unit started without a problem. I was both elated and crestfallen. I was overjoyed to have the RV back again, to see the open road and explore the unexplored, but it was also three years of going nowhere lost. I sat beside Wade in the seat and smiled; it was good to hear the purr of that engine again.

The problem with being burned by a vehicle is that you never trust it again. My spirit longs to travel far-off distances, and yet I remember the humiliation and fear of breaking down by the side of the road.

Wade says we should be cautious and take day trips to lakes that are close by, just to be sure the RV is running in perfect condition again.

Me, I want to see where the road ends, if it ends at all.

My family has grown and changed. I have grown and changed. My kids are no longer small children who sit in the back of the car with eyes wide opened to see a mountain goat. They have replaced, "Are we there yet?" with "Can I have a turn with the Gameboy?" and "What do you want to watch now on the portable DVD player?"

My older son has replaced all his adventures of travel with food. Everyplace we have been, Zack can recall the place by what he ate. It really is most remarkable.

"Do you remember coming off the boat in Prince Rupert after the whale watch? Remember the humpback whales?" we would ask Zack.

"Hmmm. Moby Dick restaurant. They had delicious calamari."

"How about when we went to Vancouver Island and saw the starfish in the shallow water by the dock in Campbell River? Do you remember that?"

"Hmmm. Best Western complementary breakfast. I had a bowl of hot cereal, two muffins with cream cheese, a coffee, two glasses of orange juice, three yogurts, and a bagel. It was so good."

(See what I mean?) I remember the grey misted sky over the ocean. The view from our room, overlooking the endless vastness of water. The eagles that dove from the treetops and skimmed the water for fish. I remember how happy I was there. It felt like that in all my travels. I had returned to a place that once was my home. I belonged there. It had become a part of me.

My son? Oh, no, he remembers food! Not that I blame him because on my first stop at the Comfort Inn in Victoria, I had my first taste of island yogurt. To this day I am haunted by the rich, creamy breakfast delicacy. I can still taste the yogurt on my tongue. It came in wonderful flavors like orange, raspberry, strawberry, vanilla, peach, and blueberry. I tested them all, that day.

Whenever I dream of my happy place, island yogurt is usually there, and chocolate, but that's a whole other story. Both delicacies are usually handfed to me by some gorgeous Irish God who wears a loincloth and has a great name like Odin or Finn. The gorgeous male may look like my husband, but isn't actually him. *Note to my husband: "Sorry, honey."

Wade and I have wonderful adventures. From the day we met, to the places we had traveled, to the sights we have seen. We have camped in tents, slept in our van, bought an RV, and stayed in hotels. Wherever we are, wherever we go, we have fun. By all means vacations should be fun.

"Just be happy, wherever you are," my dad often told me.

In February 2007, my father found out he had bone cancer. It had spread throughout his entire body, and soon he developed pneumonia. In March, just five weeks after he found out cancer was in his body, my family buried my father.

I don't think there are enough words in the English language to describe the pain and sorrow I feel, the emptiness and suffering that is consuming me. My father was only sixty-six years of age, and I am not even forty.

I wanted my final words from my father to be that be he loved me just the way I am: an artist, a writer, a good mother, a loving wife, and a faithful daughter. He didn't. I thought he might say he was sorry for all the years he tried to change me and make me into someone else he could respect. He didn't. I thought he might finally realize that I was very intelligent and creative, that maybe he saw the value in that now. He didn't.

I told my father my final words. A simplified version of Shakespeare's *King Lear*. I leaned in and whispered in my father's ear.

"I love you no more than I should, and no less than I should. For you are my father, my king, and I am a dutiful daughter."

In return I heard my father's final words.

"Gina, the lord is here. The lord is here," my dad lifted his hands to the ceiling of the hospital room.

"Is he, Dad?" I spoke through choked sobs. I could hear my heart breaking in my chest.

"Yes, and he wants a tomato." (Dad was on some pretty powerful pain killers)

I stopped for a moment and looked at my husband on the other side of the hospital bed. He had the same surprised expression on his face that I had on mine.

"Tell Wade to go behind the garage and pick a nice size tomato," Dad looked at me.

"What do I do?" Wade whispered.

"Go to the grocery store and pick up a tomato," I said.

Fast as if his feet had wings, Wade drove to the grocery store that was only three minutes away and picked up the nicest tomato he could find.

My father gulped it down as if it were the first time he ever tasted one. I was happy to be able to give my father that one thing he asked of me, a gift of a red, juicy tomato.

My father, the Poodle and El Cheapo, was gone like the flicker of a candle. It was blown out. We learn so many things from our parents. Like how to walk and talk. We are advised where the place for the best education is. Where to get the car serviced. What makes a good career. What kind of home you should buy. I mean the amount of education we receive from our parents is endless, but I think of all the things my father had passed to me in his wisdom is that you don't have to vacation in Africa, or Egypt, or Hawaii. Adventure and travel can happen in your own back yard, as long as you have someone to travel with. As long as there is someone to love, and just as long as you are being loved.

My dad didn't understand me, but that is ok. He knew me and that was enough.

My memories of the years of travelling with my family are my gifts from God. I know in my old years I can remember each and every moment with a smile and gladness in my heart.

My dad, the original, the one and only king of the campsite. The expert on shortcuts and fresh berry bushes. The man who thought pine trees were the most beautiful tree on the planet. The man who devoured every breakfast item in the hotel café because it was a complementary breakfast and said for $150 a night, they owed it to him. My father, a gentle, quiet giant, and a peacemaker.

My mother, the planner and hotel picker. The woman to whom I owe so much of my adventures.

My brother and sister, my travel companions. Bell-bottom jeans and Tonka cars with wild eyed squirrels.

And now there is a new generation of campers.

My sons, the joy of my life. The two lives I have produced and educated, laughed and smiled with. My comedians and protectors.

Now the king's crown is passed to my husband, Wade. The reason I wake up every morning and breathe. The man I fell in love with seventeen years ago, and keep finding new ways to fall in love. The new king of the campsite and fishing lakes, and well … fish in general.

My parents, my husband, my children, and someday my grandchildren. So many memories past, and still so many to come. I welcome them all, and the next King of the Campsite.

THE END

As soon as my father was buried, my mother decided that she no longer wanted to live on the farm. Not without Dad. I can't say I blame her, as Dad's spirit seemed to be everywhere we looked. It seemed that he was almost haunting us.

"If I sell, I have to clean up this place", Mom pointed out to me the cracked paint on the walls and the holes in the drywall, "It will have to have a major overhaul"

I agreed. My father was a devoted farmer, but lousy when it came to house repairs. Over the years so much had been left to decay and rot, never really fixed but just enough to make due.

I stepped in to help. I brought out my paint brushes, rollers, and staining gloves and got to work. It had been four long months of painting the top floor of the house, staining cabinets, doors and trimming. Outside my husband and sons cleaned over thirty truck loads of garbage and still there was more to be done. I never realized that when my family volunteered to help, we would be the only ones working. My brother and sister, were unavailable- too busy to pitch in. After four months of constant work everyday, I was tired and I needed a rest.

"Let's go to Jasper. Just overnight", I begged my husband, "I need to get out of here for awhile"

"Ok", my husband agreed, "We could all use a break"

During the renovations, I would sometimes stop and remember that my father just died and I would burst out crying halfway into painting a wall. I never felt like I was given time to grieve. I needed it. Even if it was for just one night, I needed to find my father in the mountains he loved so much and cry for him.

Wade and I decided to make our reservations at the Best

Western in Hinton, AB. A lovely community just outside the Jasper park gates. Having stayed there once before, we felt it would be suitable for a one night stop.

I have developed a theory about my vacations. I can pretty much tell how things are going to turn out just from the first few moments of checking into a hotel. Now just from the first few moments of checking into THIS hotel I knew there were going to be a few problems on my mini vacation.

"That's $145 for two people", the lady from behind the desk smiled at me.

"No. You've made a mistake. That should be double occupancy for four people", my husband corrected her.

"Oh, I see what happened. You checked into a double occupancy room, but failed to state there were four people in the room. That's no problem. I'll just correct this for you," the lady smiled and tapped her keyboard, fixing the numbers on the monitor, "That'll be $179"

Sometimes when I try to do the right thing, it comes around and bites me on the ass. I turned around and looked at my caboose. Yep, it had an extra lump already. I knew from that moment that this mini vacation was going to encounter a few problems. Nevertheless, there are some things that you can do nothing to change so you might as well just accept it and accepting the room that you were grossly overcharged for is one of those things. I mean what are your options here, you either pay for the room or sleep in your car. We decided to pay for the room.

With the room key in hand we drove around to the back of the hotel and parked. We opened the door and unpacked, quickly and quietly. The next item on our list , was where to eat.

This is a major problem for the people in my family. Wade and Zack eat meat. Ryan and I are vegetarians. A large percent of the restaurants out there cater to the meat eaters of the world, and leave us vegetarians hungry. Oh sure, the restaurants will say they have something for everyone, but it's usually a garden salad and a rice patty burger. All of this is a lie to fool the public that they can feed all types of people who walk through the door, but they can't. As a vegetarian I can't count how many salads I had to eat because there was nothing else-not to mention that after a thousand bowls of salad you get quite bored quite fast. The other option is the meatless burger. A cheap product of pressed rice into the shape of a burger, covered with toppings so you can't taste how bad it really is.

I feel sorry for my husband. Wade has been a professional chef for 24 years, and eating out is an extension of his business. Discovering new places, new foods, new décor is as exciting to Wade as winning a million dollar lottery ticket. For Ryan and I , though, a new restaurant can be something to be weary of because of our meatless diet.

"Let's just go to Boston Pizza", Ryan stated, "We can get any kind of pasta there"

My poor husband looked wistfully out the windows of the car as we passed new and exciting restaurants. Finally with a sigh he pulled into the Boston Pizza parking lot and parked.

There is something magical whenever my family gathers around the table. The laughter over the obvious, silly, or serious becomes infectious. Obvious observations become topics of conversation, even if the point is insignificant Whenever I sit down at the table with my family, I see the years fly by. My sons who once squirmed in high chairs and wore their food instead of eating it now steal side glances at passing girls and talk about their future careers. I think every parent feels that desire and hunger to want their children to be more successful than they are. I know I do. When I sit at the table and listen to all their future plans I know they probably will do better than me. This type of acknowledgement comforts me and frightens me. I am comforted in the knowledge that I raise two productive, creative people in this world who will make a contribution to better society. Yet I am frightened in the fact that by doing this they must move away. Leave home. The laughter that I had come to depend on whenever we sat down together will be silenced. When I think of my sons as the babies they once were and the men they are now, I know that the time will be short and they will be gone. I ate my pasta slowly, hoping to reverse time somehow. I needed to hang on just a little longer.

I don't know what possesses hotel personnel into thinking that if you are a family with teenagers then you will want to be with other families with teenagers. When we got back from lunch that is exactly what happened. In the rooms beside us, two families moved in with seven children ranging in ages from 17 to 10. Normally I would say that children are expected to behave as children, but in a public place I demand my sons are gentlemen and act as such. Pity, no one told the family next door the rules for public places. The new family went out their way to be rude, obtuse, loud, and careless of thought for anyone else in the building as they pounded on the walls, yelled at each other through the doors, and ran up and down the hallways.

I looked at my sons sitting quietly on the bed playing their gameboys. I was proud of them in that moment. They were true gentlemen as they quietly talked to each other. How long that would last, I don't know .

A person never knows when disaster is about to strike. You can be just walking along without a care in the world and BAM! A piano falls on you. Or you can be driving down a deserted street when all of a sudden WOOSH! The dam breaks open and the street is now a river, and your car is now a boat, and you have to paddle with your hands to reach the stop sign to make a left turn. For me, disaster struck at 1 o'clock in the morning and it would be in my bathroom. I woke up and groggily took my weary body over to use the facilities. I flushed the toilet and to my horror the water rose up and over the bowl and quickly spread across the floor.

"Oh Wade. Help!", I yelled.

My husband jumped out of bed and ran to the door.

"What the hell did you do?", he asked me as water slipped under his feet.

"I don't know. It must be plugged somewhere. Help me!", I begged

"What are we going to do?"

"I don't know. We have to empty the bowl so it will stop flooding"

"With what, Gina?"

"I don't know. Find something! A scoop of some kind"

Wade and I walked into the bedroom and quickly surveyed our room. A coffee pot, a set of four glasses, a set of four cups, and a small trash can. The coffee pot just seemed wrong somehow, the cups were too small, and the trash can was too large. Now what?

"Hurry, Wade. We have to do something", I jumped onto the rug as the water now spilled under the door , across the bedroom vanity area, and into a closet.

"Here, use this", Wade handed me an orange plastic bowl from our picnic set. I studied the dish for a moment thinking I should burn a symbol on this thing that it should never again be used for human consumption. I watched with horror as the water continued to pour over the edge of the bowl. I grabbed the dish and started bailing. Finally, it seemed the water went down. I breathed a sigh of relief over one crisis that seemed to be solved. However, there was still the matter of the flooded floor.

"Grab the towels", I suggested

Wade and I grabbed all the towels off the racks and started to pat the floor dry again, carefully wringing out the water in the bathtub.

"Well, there goes my shower in the morning", I gave Wade a little smile.

"Don't worry honey. It's late. I'm tired. Let's go to bed and I'll get a plunger from the front desk in the morning"

I crawled into bed and slept. I didn't notice the hard bed or the air conditioner blasting away all night, the long weary night of toilet wrestling was too much for me. I was tired. It was 7:30 am when I awoke. I stretched and rolled out of bed and headed to the bathroom. Last night's toilet calamity was still fresh on my mind when my feet walked into two inches of water.

"Wade! Wade!", I heard myself yelling again. I had a strong sense of Dejavu as if I had been here in this situation already once before.

"What the hell?", Wade growled at me.

"It must of flowed over in the middle of the night",

In fact it had. I grabbed a still wet towel from the bathtub and started mopping the floor. The plastic dish was again dunked into the toilet bowl and used for bailing. A steady stream poured over the edge and soaked the bathroom floor, the vanity area, the closet and part of the rug.

"Oh no", I muttered, "We have to get help"

Wade quickly got dressed and ran to the front desk. It's funny how small things, unimportant things, can sudden become a valuable tool in a crisis. Well, in this crisis the plunger seemed to glow with a golden aura around it. I felt like a pygmy native who had never before seen a rubber cup attached to a stick. It was perfect in its design. Flawless. A gift from the Gods. I didn't know whether to dip it in the bowl or sacrifice a goat in its honor. Wade opted for the toilet bowl as there were no goats available in our room at 7:30 in the morning.

Two small plunges and the toilet flushed. It was a miracle. I carefully rung out the towels and neatly placed them in the bathtub. I shuttered to think where they were all night but it was an emergency.

One thing I hate about Hotel rooms, besides the high cost of the room, the hard beds, noisy air conditioners and neighbor,s is the packing up. First I check the bathroom, the vanity, the dressers, the closet, the beds and the floor. When I've checked every place, I check it all over again, and again, and again. I am, if nothing else, very thorough.

It was outside , while packing up the car, that we ran into the noisy neighbors. They decided at 8:00 in the morning to wake up their travelling companions by shouting at them through the key hole. I couldn't believe the audacity of these people. They had absolutely no regard for anyone else in the building.

"Perhaps they think they are providing a courtesy call", I told my youngest son as they walked by.

I raised my sons to always think of others, and themselves last. I think we have entered a society of teaching our children, "Do whatever makes you happy –even if it causes someone else misery. You are number one". I was never raised that way, and I can't raise my kids to believe that. I wanted my sons to have courage, be respected, have grace, be admired, and above all else be a gentleman. I think I have accomplished that as my sons open the doors for ladies, pull out chairs, and rise from the table waiting for a lady to sit down. They hang back and let other people who were there first serve themselves at a lunch counter, and refuse to fight back when bullied or threatened.

Perhaps I did too well of a job as I watched the noisy family swoop into the breakfast room and cut in front of my sons and help themselves to coffee, tea, toast, cereal, bagels, and fruit. My boys stood on the side and let the family pass. My family all exchanged looks of disgust in other people's manners and walked forward to the counter, only to be cut off again by the noisy family. With four adults and seven children, they came in constant waves, back and forth to the breakfast counter.

"Boys. Come sit down. There is nothing we can do until they pass", I whispered to my sons and sat down at a nearby table.

It was only my husband, whom I never trained for grace or respect who was able to shove the noisy family to one side and grab his breakfast. I looked at my sons and then to the noisy family. They seemed to be gobbling down, tea, juice, coffee, bagels, fruit, cereal, and muffins while my family had only tea and a muffin. So what was the lesson here? I thought to myself. I guess in the gene pool of life, we would die – except for Wade. If you teach your children respect, they starve. If you teach your children to be obnoxious they feast.

I imagined my husband as a fat, lazy lion in Africa. He'd probably fart a lot because he doesn't exercise and he'd never find the laundry hamper which is right in front of him. He would probably develop a cute, little bald spot on the top of his mane because he wears baseball caps constantly and it would etch a hole up there. Somehow, he would manage to get away from the TV set and hunt for food. Wade would never be without food.

I had paid $179 for a room with a flooded floor, no shower, disrespectful neighbors and now no breakfast. I was on the fast track to disgusted.

I remember once a few years ago, my family took my parents to a trip to Cold Lake. We had arrived at a bad time. There was a military air show going on and all the hotel, motels, and Inns were booked solid. It took almost all day, but we finally managed to find two available rooms for the night. We were sandwiched between two foreign military units. All night long it was silent. We never herd a peep from anyone, until 5:00 in the morning when they started pounding on all the doors and yelled at all the soldiers to get up and out of bed.

"On the Deck!", someone pounded on my door.

I got up and opened the door a crack."No I won't", I looked up into the face of a young officer, "I will not stand on any deck for any country at 5:00 in the morning. Although I love my country and I place my hand over my heart when the flag is waving, I even put a flag in my yard to show my pride, I still will not let anyone see my pajamas, except my husband. I'm an old fashioned girl that way"

"Oh Sorry", the officer blushed.

When we all woke up at a more respectful hour, we mad our way out to the van and started to pack up. My father and my husband went into the office to return the hotel key. When the men came back out they informed the rest of us that the hotel served a complimentary breakfast.

"That hotel cost me $139 a night. I am going to eat everything they got. They owe it to me", my Dad announced and sat down at a table and did just that. He ate half a loaf of bread, a small box of cereal, a bowl of hot cereal, three muffins, and two cups of coffee. Dad then poured himself two cups of orange juice, and took fruit for the road.

I guess I am like my father, because that hotel in Hinton took my money and I wanted something back for the money I spent. I planned to eat a full breakfast. I wanted to eat everything they had. Instead, I had to settle for tea and a muffin. I felt deflated, and oddly still hungry.

I felt as though my vacation had been spoiled by this loathsome family who were on their way back home to Vancouver. I know this for a fact. In fact everyone in the breakfast room knew this information as they shouted their driving plans back and forth to each other across the room. I am never a vindictive person. I never wish another human being ill will…unless they deserve it. I closed my eyes and asked God to please pop their tire in the middle of the highway miles from nowhere. I felt God owed me at least that much.

I was happy to return to the open road again. The chatter and excitement as we headed towards the Jasper park gates filled our car, like musical notes.

"How long are you staying?", the young man in the booth asked us as we parked under the window.

"Just for the day", my husband stated and opened his wallet.

"That'll be $17.99 plus tax"

"But it's just for a few hours", Wade frowned.

"It's still considered a day pass and it will be $17.99 plus tax"

Wade and I looked at each other and paid the attendant. With a sigh we passed through the gates and continued down the highway. I felt as if we had been robbed. Our day had not even begun and already half our budget was gone and we were running low on gas. I had planned a trip in a lovely hotel, places of interest, retrace past camping trips, but I guess it just wasn't meant to be. We had to stick around Jasper and go home.

Ryan had found a brochure the night before and saw an ad for a gondola ride. The same gondola ride, that my father befriended a marmot on, and insisted that the forestry room was just a path. The ad said the marmots were still on the mountain, as well as the gift shop. I wanted to take my sons there, like my father did for me when I was a girl. I thought it was the perfect place to honor him, to talk to the clouds, to be near to heaven as I could get.

Slowly our car wound up the steep hill and into a parking lot. We got out and walked through the courtyard and looked at the prices by the ticket counter. When I was a young girl, my father paid $23.99 for all five of us to ride to the top of the mountain. I couldn't believe my eyes. I was in shock. The tickets were now $24.00 per person. For all four of us to ride to the top of the mountain, it would cost us $100.00, plus tax.

"This is exploiting the tourists!", I exclaimed out loud, "This is a example of exploiting the rich and a punishment to the middle class and poor"

"It's ok", Ryan looked at me sadly, "I understand"

I looked back my son, and my heart broke. I didn't want him to understand. I wanted to take him up the mountain. I wanted my sons to see what I was once privileged to see with my family. Instead my patronage to my dad and my children was shattered like glass hitting a sidewalk.

We back down the hill to explore the town of Jasper instead. My father always taught me, "When life gives you lemons- make lemonade". I decided to do that, for Dad's sake.

My family strolled in and out of the many little shops. There was so much to see. Funny t-shirts, postcards, native paintings, native masks, ornamental bowls and boxes, flags, jewelry, and even homemade candy.

Once when my family went to Drumheller to explore the museum, we dropped into the local gift shop. I left with a pair of native crafted earrings of orca whales, and my husband left with a dinosaur pen that lights up when you write with it. This sort of thing has been going on for ages, so my children were not surprised to see that I left the gift shop in Jasper with a painting of a loon with its spirit symbol in the water, a painting that really moved me. Nor were the children surprised when Wade left the shop with two postcards and candy.

On our way out of the park we stopped by Maligne Canyon. An impressive display, of narrow jagged cliffs , with a rushing river on the stone floor. There were six bridges (or stages) that you can choose to walk on. If you choose the first two stages you will have toured the canyon for fifteen minutes. Since we all felt so horribly robbed of a trip, we decided to tour the entire six stages. We didn't care how long it took. In fact the longer the better, we thought.

I watched my sons ahead of me, as they graciously let hikers move past them or the elderly grab the rails to get better footing. Once in a while the rock would jut out to a steep step, and my sons would hold my hands tightly and guide me to the step below. The hike was breathtaking as we followed the river as it cut though the stone walls. Swirling, and pouring faster and faster as we moved down the mountain trail. The ferns and green moss grew on the cliffs as tall pine trees created a lush, green forest.

We walked past boulders, benches, and over bridges through the forest and down the mountain until the rail that securely held you back from the cliff…vanished.

"I don't like this. I want to go back", I told my family.

I just had this terrible vision of one us (probably me), falling down the cliff and being lost in the river forever.

"Fine", Wade grunted and we headed back up the trail again.

I knew it was a disappointment to the guys that I insisted we turn back, but I couldn't shake the feeling that someone would get hurt if we continued. I just had to go back.

There is often a problem when you constantly walk down a mountain, at some point you have to walk back up again. I felt the muscles in my legs scream at stage four. My ankles felt weak and they were about to give out at stage three. My heart raced and wanted to jump out of my chest and stage two. I couldn't walk another step and had to sit on a bench at stage one. I was near medical help when I finally made it back to the car. Never in my , whole life was I happy to travel four hours back home, resting my carcass.

The walk was beautiful, haunting and mysterious. It will long live in my memory as a place of wonder. We sadly looked to each other in the car. The trip was over. It was time to go home.

Two days later we went shopping at the mall. My husband came out of one of the stores laughing. From his bag he produced a plunger.

"We'll carry it in the trunk where ever we go", Wade smiled.

"It's what I always wanted", I gushed.

I thought about it on the way home. I hope I don't have to carry that plunger overseas. I could just imagine the faces of the custom officials as they x-rayed my luggage.

"Good Lord, Phil! It that a plunger in her luggage bag?"

"I believe it is Bob"

At first it would be a shock to them to see a plunger being pushed through customs, but then I imagined it would be a source of amusement as the officials would invite everyone in the airport to view my x-ray over coffee and donuts.

"Maybe she has rectum problems", the Stewardess would laugh

"Mighty big problem if she's carrying an entire plunger with her", the pilot would reply

"Maybe it's for pygmy natives who never saw a plunger before", someone would add

"What a remarkable woman. Giving a plunger to heal the world", the pilot would nod his head in reflection.

On better thought, next time I make hotel reservations, I'll ask for a plunger and extra towels to be delivered to my room before I even get there.

A week had passed. The hotel did not work out as we had planned. I needed a break from rolling paint, and the stress of a grieving family. Wade and I decided a day at the lake is what we needed. A quiet little place to let the worries and frustrations just drift out on the water. I had the perfect place in mind. Bellis Lake.

Bellis Lake is only 10 km east from Smokey Lake, AB. A quiet little lake, that is only 1/2km long and wide. The campground is usually quiet. That is every time I had been there , there were only four or five campers in the entire campsite. I love it there, the serenity and peacefulness of such a lovely place. The campground offers tables, a fire pit, an outhouse, water pump, and a day camp area. I think what I love the best is the tall evergreen trees that shade and protect you while you sit in quiet contemplation and the haunting call of the loon birds as they search the water for fish.

The common loon is my favorite bird. I love their sharp beaks, the black and white speckled feathers, the sleek long neck and fuzzy little black babies. I love how they glide effortlessly through the water, but their call - that mysterious, haunting call. Once you hear it, it is a sound that stays with you always. There is no other bird or animal that makes that eerie sound…it is quite spiritual. I waited all winter in the gloom of the snow and cold. I waited all spring as the sun slowly warmed the earth. It was summer and I could wait no longer to hear them cry out across the lake once more.

Now that I have mentioned all the wonderful things I love about Bellis Lake, now I will mention what I don't like about Bellis lake. There is a flight of steps that lead down a steep embankment to the shore line. There are roughly twenty steps, now I know you are asking yourself, What is the big deal with that? Well, the bid deal is those twenty steps are like a thousand steps when you are carrying a 101 lb canoe, two inflatable rafts, four paddles, four life jackets, a fishing rod, a fishing box, a minnow net, and pulling a 95 lb dog. Wade and I have mastered this feat with master precision over the years. Never once , dumping the canoe, kids, or dog.

Ryan guided his raft into the knee deep water and climbed in and started to paddle. He didn't paddle well, but sometimes you have to let kids figure out things so they can help themselves. Zack sat in his raft on the shoreline. I don't know what the purpose of that was, but he was happy there.

I wrestled with our dog, Jade, for ten minutes to please sit down in the front of the canoe. I petted her , I spoke softly to her until she was calm again. Inch by inch, Wade pushed the canoe out into the water and we paddled away from the shore line. I love canoeing. I love being on the water. I love the fact that there are no people. No worries. No phones. No tv. And no land to hold be back from being truly free. There is just you and the water. Wade and I glided across the lake and slowly turned around to encourage our eldest son to come join his family on the water. This encouragement lasted twenty minutes.

Then we heard a call for help. It was our youngest son, Ryan.

"What now?" , Wade grumbled in the back of the boat ,"I guess I won't go fishing today"

"Yes, you will. We came to go fishing and we will go fishing, but we have to save Ryan first"

We turned the canoe around and paddled across the lake towards our son who was turning himself in circles on the water.

"What are you doing?", I asked Ryan when we pulled up beside him.

"I only have one paddle and I can't go forward or backward", Ryan explained.

"Ryan , you have to paddle on one side and then switch and paddle on the other side"

"Oh God, that will take me all day", Ryan groaned, "I hate this. I want another paddle"

"We'll get you one, but not now. There is no Walmart in the middle of the lake"

Just then out of the corner of my eye, I saw my eldest son floating aimlessly by on his raft.

"Oh Geez", I groaned, "Wade, we better go get him before he hits the reeds"

"Who cares if he does. Let him", Wade replied

"If Zack goes in the reeds, he'll get stuck in there and I am not going through the muck to get him loose"

"Fine, we'll turn the boat around and go get him. I guess I won't go fishing today"

"Stop that! You will get to fish but let's get the kids sorted out first, so we can enjoy ourselves"

Wade and I turned the boat around again and went to save Zack. I nicknamed my eldest son, Otter. Otters are an animal that love to play, they seem to never have any worries or stress. They just lay on the kelp and eat shell fish all day. Otters are not hard workers, they don't build damns like a beaver, or pick up sticks to build a nest like a bird, otters just let life be. My son, Zack, is an otter. He just rather float around aimlessly than paddle his way from a life threatening crisis of falling over a water fall. He doesn't make his own supper or dinner, he'd rather starve himself until I come home to make him sandwich. The only thing that my son does , is laundry and reading. Everyday Zack gathers all the laundry in the house and has them cleaned and folded, and ready to be put away. The only other habit of Zack's is reading. I usually find my son in his room. The shelves are filled with comic books, mythology, animal encyclopedias, assorted classical novels and the entire series of The Lord of the Rings. My son is a smart boy, a natural scientist. He is also very lazy and the child that I rescue the most. I tried many times to let my son figure things out for himself, but it sometimes becomes too painful to watch. I only hope he marries a nice girl with sharp, pointed boots that will kick some sense into him.

Wade and I pulled Zack to shore with a rope and tied him to the back of our canoe and went back out on the water, with Zack floating behind to go save Ryan.

Ryan is the opposite of Zack. Ryan is more adventurous, more willing to take risks and can make his own sandwich. Ryan is ambitious, clever, and has already made plans to graduate Highschool when he is 16 . He hopes to get a full time job and earn experience so he can run his own business someday. Ryan never needs my help, but once in a blue moon he does. When that occasion arises, I plan to always be there for him.

"Wade, turn the canoe around", I started to paddle.

"Geez, I am never going to fish", Wade growled.

"We have to go save Ryan". I was starting to get mad. We came to fish and paddle around the lake. So far we have spent ten minutes getting the dog to sit in the canoe, twenty minutes getting Zack in the raft, ten minutes tying Zack to the back of the canoe and now we were off to rescue Ryan.

"I don't want to tie to the back of you", Ryan frowned at me.

"Just do it!", I yelled. Kids and dogs were proving too much for me. My last nerve was about to snap.

"Well, how am I going to fish with the kids behind me? I might catch one of them", explained Wade.

"JUST FISH!!!", I yelled. I had enough. My arms were burning from the paddling around the lake, going from one kid to another with a grouchy husband behind me, and a wiggling dog.

"Fine", Wade gruffed and dropped his line gently into the lake. His first attempt at a fish was green weeds. From behind the canoe I heard the boys snicker and laugh at their father's funny green fish.

He dropped his line a few more times until I heard it, "Uh, Oh"

I hate the word, "Uh, oh". It is never associated with anything good.

"What is it?", I questioned.

"My line is caught on this net", replied Wade.

"I'll get you untangled", I told him. I have a job when I fish with Wade. It is my job to paddle the canoe while Wade trolls his line behind the canoe. It is also my job to put worms on the hook, look for marshmallows in the little jars, and untangle his line when he is caught. With as must speed as I could muster I got Wade separated from the net with only one hook remaining, in order to do this I had to first unclip the lead from the pole.

"Thanks Geanie", my husband praised me as he took back his rod and line.

I love being in the front of the canoe. I can see the whole view in front of me. I see trees, and the sparkle of the sun on the water. I can only see nature. I can't see the two boys behind me play fighting with plastic paddles or my husband wrestling with fishing rods and weeds at the bottom of the lake bed. That is why it is always disturbing when you hear your husband yelling behind you.

"No!, No!", Wade yelled.

I carefully turned around to face my husband. His face was twisted with anguish, his hands were just dangling above the water, and there was no trace of net, rod, or fishing line.

"What happened?", I asked.

"I went to snap the lead back on the pole and I lost my grip and my rod sunk in the water", Wade explained.

We sat there for a moment. Perhaps it was a silence for the rod that was never going to fish again. Perhaps it was a silent respect for the fish that won over another fisherman's rod. Or perhaps it was just a silence of the moment. There was nothing more that could be done.

"Well, let's go home and have some hot dogs", I told my husband.

Like I said, there was nothing more that could be done. It is amazing how short a fishing trip can be when you lose your fishing rod in the lake. It defeats the whole purpose of being there, somehow.

With a lot of effort, we made it back to shore and walked up the stairs. Carrying all our gear and dragging the dog we made it back to the truck.

'As soon as I can, I am going to get you boys new paddles for your boats", I said.

"Yeah, especially since we can't go on dragging you both around the lake forever", said Wade.

"Why not?", asked Zack," I like it"

My Zack, always the otter.

"You won't drag me around. I'll paddle myself", Ryan spoke up.

I patted my son on the shoulder and gave him a little smile, "I know you will son", I said softly, "I know you will"

I was sad to leave Bellis Lake that day. Like always, there was only one couple who came to the lake to enjoy a picnic. We were virtually alone. I rested my head against the truck door frame as the men tied up the canoe and threw our equipment in the truck box. Just as I opened my door, I heard it. It was what I came for. The loons called out across the lake. That haunting, mysterious , beautiful, eerie call. It made the whole trip worthwhile.

Somewhere between childhood and adult we lose our youth. That innocence, that which keeps us young. Luckily that is why we have children. Children are the source to staying young, and keeping a good sense of humor. I don't need anti wrinkle cream or the lost fountain of youth , I have my sons to keep me young and active. They make me laugh. I hope I have a lot of laugh lines in my life time, what a wonderful badge that would be to wear.

When I was a girl, I had my father- the king of the campsite. My father has been gone for ten months now and the house is almost fully renovated, but the ability to appreciate the small moments on vacation is still with me. My dad was a whole other person when we camped. He went from serious farmer, to light hearted traveler. I loved my father in these moments. He gave me some of the most wonderful memories, that can fill several novels. Like the time he told me that sunscreen was a waste of money and canola oil can do just as well a job. I laughed when my father showed me his legs. They were so shiny soaked with canola oil , I am sure the Hubble telescope could pick it up. Then there was the time Dad had cut on his finger and went through the medicine cabinet looking for Pollysporin Ointment Cream only to accidently put hemorrhoid cream all over his hands. "Wow, but this feels good on the bones", dad said and spread hemorrhoid cream all over his knees, ankles and elbows.

Now my father's legacy lives in me. What my father loved , is now mine to give my family. No matter where we live, and what we chose to do with our lives, Dad will want us to continue. With love, hope and faith, I know we will.

ABOUT THE AUTHOR

Gina Bolton is known as an artist, a singer, a muscian, a master gardener, and a writer. She is a member of the Writer's Guild of Alberta, and has printed stories of her experiences in life and poetry with the Edmonton Journal and various magazines.

Known as a multi-talented woman, Gina has sold her paintings in galleries, sang to audiences,worked for large franchise companies as their garden expert, and now will delight her readers with her first debut book.

Gina lives in Redwater, Ab Canada with her husband, and two teenage sons, a dog, two cats, and four goldfish.

Printed in the United States
110039LV00005B/78/P